The Journey
of Discovering Inner Peace

Christina Samycia, PsyD

Christina Samycia PsyD, Ltd.

www.christinasamyciapsyd.com

The Journey of Discovering Inner Peace/ Christina Samycia, PsyD —1st ed.
ISBN 978-1-09830-416-4

"For those who desire to heal themselves and the world"

Imagine feeling free: freedom from your thoughts, your feelings, and external circumstances.

Imagine feeling empowered; knowing that no matterwhat situation you are in, everything will be ok.

Imagine feeling joy; creating the life you want, not bound by fear or guilt.

Imagine feeling safe:
feeling connected to the world around you.

Imagine feeling love,
compassion, and forgiveness in
your heart.

This is inner peace.

Introduction

We are all wounded. No matter who we are, where we come from, what our stories are, we have all endured emotional pain and carry the scars from our life journey. No matter what our gender, race, socio-economic status, we all suffer. We all experience sadness, anxiety, anger, hopelessness, resentment, and health issues. Our wounds are what we all share. Because we are spiritual beings having a human experience in this material world, we all have a duality. As humans, we experience emotional and physical pain. But we can transcend our suffering by healing and rewriting our story and reconnecting to the feelings of love, connection and peace that are spiritually inherent in all of us.

On our journey here, we are all trying our best to cope with the suffering that comes with the human experience. All of us, to some extent, seek to escape our pain either through maladaptive coping mechanisms, such as the pursuit of pleasure, avoidance, minimization, or distorting reality. But no matter how much we try to escape, our pain is still there. However, some of us have this inner voice; this inner knowing that speaks to us. This voice compels us to dig deeper and to look at our pain and dysfunctional dynamics because on some level, we know we can transcend them. Hopefully, this book will help you along your journey of discovering inner peace. I applaud you for being so brave and taking this huge step toward self-discovery and healing. By doing your work, you are not only healing yourself, but you are also healing the world around you.

"No one saves us but ourselves. No one can and no one may. We ourselves must walk the path."

—Buddha

Preface

After publishing my first book, Discovering Inner Peace, I had this illusion that I had actually discovered inner peace. I did not realize that this was just the beginning of my journey and that there were so many more layers of pain that were going to surface in just a matter of time. Within a few years, I encountered a series of life altering events and found myself in a deep depression. This led me to continue my journey of self-discovery and healing. Because I had already done the work of uncovered childhood scars and understood my dysfunctional dynamics, I realized that talk therapy was just not enough. I discovered that I had not truly processed the emotional trauma from my childhood and deep pain that transcended even this lifetime. In addition to therapy, I explored various other modalities such as Neuro-emotional technique (NET), hypnosis, colorpuncture, meditation, energy work, sound therapy and so much more to help me truly heal.

As a psychologist, I find that many of us are suffering because we are not at peace in our hearts, but we can transcend our suffering and find peace by accepting that we are all wounded, healing from our past, changing our belief systems and reconnecting with our spiritual selves. I am not going to mislead you to think that inner peace is an easy thing to find. It isa commitment to the process of self-exploration and healing. Inner peace is not a destination but a journey of discovering it. I hope to inspire you tobecome empowered and take charge of your healing so that you may transcend your own suffering. As you embark on your journey, I would like to share with you some of the pieces of wisdom I discovered along the way.

Wishing you peace and love,
Christina

Philosophy of this Book

- Our childhood experiences shape our beliefs about ourselves and the world.

- Some of these experiences are accompanied by emotional pain that isn't fully processed which becomes stored in our body as cellular memory.

- In addition to childhood trauma, we have trauma stored in our DNA from our ancestors, parents, and past lives, which also influences our belief systems and amplifies our emotional pain.

- How we appraise current reality triggers pain that is already there even if we are not consciously aware of it. Unprocessed emotional pain will likely surface and can manifest as emotional and/or physical ailments.

- We have the power to change our belief systems and heal our emotional scars.

- By reconnecting to our spiritual selves and understanding why we are here, this can aid in alleviating our emotional distress.

So, let's begin!

Table of Contents

Part 1

Your Story

Understanding why you think and feel the way you do

"He who knows others is wise.
He who knows himself is enlightened."
— Lao Tsu

Introduction to Part 1

Welcome to the First Step of Your Journey!

We all have a story that we tell ourselves. When we were children, we created a belief system about ourselves and the world based on our childlike perspective, limited life experiences and the beliefs of those around us. Based on our childhood experiences, we also endured emotional pain that we haven't fully processed, which is stored within our physical body. This story and the emotions attached to it becomes the building block of our cognitive and emotional foundation. We also have other information from our ancestors, parents and past lives stored in our DNA that reinforce our story. Most of us rarely question this story about ourselves or the beliefs that we hold. We do not always understand that there is an inaccurate script that is playing in our subconscious mind, which defines who we are, influences our lives and motivates our decisions. This story shapes our perceptions, triggers emotional pain and we attract experiences that reinforce it. Unless we understand this story, process our emotional pain, and rewrite it, we are trapped by it. However, we can become the authors of our livesby understanding and rewriting our story. This book can help you geta better understanding of why you are in pain and some suggestions on how to transcend your suffering to help you find inner peace. This book combines various theories and practices, both psychological and spiritual, to help you along your journey of self-discovery and healing. I am so excited to be able to provide you with some wisdom to help you as you travel along your journey of discovering inner peace.

"Who looks outside, dreams; who looks inside, awakens."

—Carl Jung

Chapter 1

Your Journey Begins

**We come into the world with
a blueprint of perfection.**

From the moment we are born, our journey in this lifetimebegins. Because we are spiritual beings entering into a material body, theorists speculate that we already have basic informationand a set of belief systems that we bring into this world. We carry knowledge of our spiritual selves as well as a blueprintfor optimal health. Some of these beliefs include that we are wise, whole, connected to all, safe, unconditionally loved and immortal. Our body knows how to functional optimally and has information of how to grow and heal. We also bring in additionalinformation that is encoded in our DNA from our ancestors, parents and past lives as well as information as to what we are to learn, accomplish and experience in this lifetime. However, wedon't usually have conscious access to this information.

Our childhood experiences create a highly inaccurate foundation of how we view ourselves and the world.

Although we have an original program of perfection, once in the material body, this information becomes distorted. We begin gathering information through the experiences we encounter. We are receptive to our mother's, father's and other's feelings about us, their situations and views of the world. This is the beginning of the framework of how we view ourselves and the world. For example, if we had a narcissistic parent, we may learn that we are conditionally loved. If our parents had anxiety, we may learn that we are not safe in the world. These ideas conflict with our innate spiritual beliefs of being loved, safe and connected.

During our childhood, because of our limited cognitive capacity, we create egocentric fantasies about why things happen. These speculations become the foundation of our belief systems. For example, if our parents were conflicted about our birth, we might form a belief that we are not wanted. Or if there was animosity within the household, we may blame ourselves. Many of these concepts are inaccurate. Although some of these beliefs may be conscious, most of this informationgets stored in our subconscious mind. In addition, part of this subconscious mechanism are the biochemical and neurological response systems such as the fight or flight response attached to these experiences. These mechanisms all play a role in how our beliefs are shaped and how we respond to our environment.

As we continue to develop, we add to this framework of inaccurate belief systems and patterns of thinking and behaving, and it colors the experiences we have as we continue on our journey. These belief systems and patterns influence every aspect of our lives. They influence how we think and feel about ourselves and the world and motivates our behavior. Additionally, we have unresolved emotional needs created by our formative experiences, which also becomes part of our subconscious emotional framework. We become energetically attached to these dynamics that were unresolved in childhood and they replay in our lives. For example, if we felt conditionally loved, we may spend a lot of time and energy trying to get love and approval by overachieving or pleasing others. Or if we grew up in an unstable household, we may be overly preoccupied with needing to feel safe, which can possibly manifest in obsession and compulsive behaviors.

As we go through life and encounter situations, whether we consciously realize it or not, we appraise these situations based on some of these inaccurate belief systems. We continue to use these inaccurate paradigms, which distorts our reality because we are applying past experiences to try to explain our present reality. This is problematic because our past experiences have nothing to do with our current reality. Therefore, we do not see reality as it truly is because we use our past experiences to interpret our current reality.

Unprocessed emotions and unresolved needs from childhood are stored in cellular memory and the subconscious mind.

Our childhood experiences may trigger emotional pain such as fear, sadness, abandonment, shame, frustration, and anger.This information conflicts with our original program of feeling happy, safe, connected, and unconditionally loved. Researchers speculate that even as early as in the womb, we are receptiveto the emotions of others within our environment. As an infant, when we were sad, angry or scared, we freely expressed and processed our emotions. As we grew older, we were taught to hold our emotions in. Researcher and theorists suggest that these suppressed emotions do not go away. These emotions become encoded within our physical body as cellular memory. When we encounter situations that resemble these experiences, whether we are conscious of it or not, this triggers emotional pain that is already there. For example, if you felt that your mother was emotionally unavailable and you did not feel as though you received her love and approval, whenever you perceive rejection or abandonment, it triggers this scar. This original scar may create a lifetime of chronic depression. If you had a significant trauma at birth, such as being born with the umbilical cord wrapped around your neck, this may create a lifetime of chronic anxiety and create a belief system that the world is scary, and I am not safe.

Christina Samycia, PsyD

Suffering is internal because it is how we appraise reality and the emotions that it triggers that causes our distress.

As we travel on our life journey, we encounter situations that trigger an emotional reaction. These situations are neither "good" nor "bad" in themselves, but it is how we appraise these circumstances and the emotions it elicits that creates our distress. Although we usually blame our distress on external events, it is how we appraise these situations, consciously and subconsciously, and the emotions it elicits that cause our suffering. For example, if we do not get a job we want, it is how we appraise this that causes our suffering. We may become upset because we may misperceive that we didn't get the job because we are not good enough or because nothing ever goes our way, which triggers emotional pain. Therefore, the situation of not getting the job did not lead you to feel upset, it is how you interpreted this situation. Whether we are feeling sad, anxious, angry or whatever else is disrupting our peace, it is how we are perceiving our current life circumstances that is triggering an emotional response which is only amplifying unprocessed pain that is stored in our body. Therefore, our suffering is internally created.

Because suffering is created internally, the goal is to make changes to our perceptions, not to blame or fix external situations. External circumstances are neutral in nature. It is not until we judge them that they have meaning. These appraisals, rooted in a past reality, then triggers subconscious emotional pain; this pain is already there eliciting an emotional as well as a physical response. Again, we do not see situations as they are, but color it through the lenses of our past experiences. Be- cause unprocessed pain amplifies this experience; it is important to process it.

Here is a Buddhist proverb to illustrate this. This proverb asks us to imagine that we are a glass of water and that there is a layer of sediment at the bottom that represents past painful emotional experiences that we haven't fully processed. External situations

6

are the spoon that stirs up the water making it become cloudy. We believe the spoon clouded the water, but it didn't. If there were no sediment on the bottom, even when the spoon stirred the water, it would remain clear. Therefore, we need to clear out this sediment by working through, as much as we can, our painful experiences. We can also work on understanding that external situations may be triggering past emotional experiences in the moment and minimize our reactions, as well as process this trigger from the original trauma, which will be addressed.

We are spiritual beings having a human experience.

As Teilhard de Chardin said, "We are not human beings having a spiritual experience; we are spiritual beings having a human experience." Because you are a spiritual being within a human body, you, the essence of who you are, is what we can define as consciousness, your spirit or soul. Therefore, you are wise, connected to everything, unconditionally loved and immortal.

We all have an ego, which represents the physical or material aspect of who we are. Part of this ego is the belief system we created about ourselves based on how we interpreted a collection of events that happened to us. Our ego is a collection of thoughts, conscious and subconscious, about who we think we are, which is largely based on our childhood experiences that are highly inaccurate. However, who we are is not a collection of thoughts. Because we are not our thoughts, we are not necessarily who we think we are. This is quite a profound shift in how we probably think about ourselves because we tend to identify with who we think we are. However, if you were your thoughts, would you really be able to change your thoughts? Exactly, so, who is doing the changing? You are. You, then, are not your thoughts, if in fact you can change them. You have thoughts, as well as feelings, but they are not who you are. This may be a hard concept to grasp because we tend to identify with the thinker. You may also believe that your thoughts and feelings control you, but this is not true. You can control your

7

thoughts and feelings because you have the power to change how you think and feel.

You can look at this concept as though the ego is the participant, and you are the observer. Here is an example to illustrate this idea. You receive an email from your boss who wants to meet with you. It may be that your first reaction is to get nervousand automatically jump to the worst-case scenario. You may be-gin to think that you did something wrong and will be punished. This is part of your ego or your story. However, you as the observer, have the ability to slow down this experience and catch this thought and think and then feel something else. You can rationalize that chances are everything is ok and even if it isn't, you will be able to deal with it. You can control the thinker, who, by the way, is the one who is making you miserable. You are something much greater than who you think you are. Identifyingwith your thoughts leads you to be trapped in certain ideas aboutyourself, but at any moment, you can choose to be just be who youare. And because you are not your story, you have the power tore-write it because this story keeps you trapped in suffering.

Most of us don't realize that this spiritual part of us can be the navigating force in our lives because we tend to identify with our ego self. Inner peace is found when we allow the essence of who we are in the driver's seat, not the ego. Although we need an ego to navigate our world, it is important to not allow the ego to define who we are. Part of the work we will do is reconnectingyou to your spiritual self instead of being defined by your ego selfand making corrections to this ego construct you created. Being more connected to your spiritual self is helpful in transcending emotional pain and helping you in changing belief systems to one's that are more positive and empowering.

You have the power to change your belief systems, heal your emotional pain and rewrite your story.

The good news is, you have the power to change these belief systems on both a conscious and subconscious level and process the trauma that is stored in your cellular memory and feel at peace, which is inherent in all of us. You have the power to change how you appraise your reality and to determine better ways of coping and responding to these situations. You are probably not aware that you created belief systems based on your childhood experiences, which are highly inaccurate and that you can change them at any time. It is so important to understand that many of the stress producing beliefs about yourself and the world are not necessarily true because these beliefs were created in childhood with your child-like lenses and limited life experiences.

Although you created a story about yourself and the world, you have the power to rewrite your story and update your beliefs. I will be offering you tools to help you understand your story, detach from it and how to rewrite it. I will also provide you with some suggestions for new belief systems you may consider adding to your life as well as how to heal your emotional pain. Re- writing your story and changing your belief systems will be ad- dressed on both a conscious and subconscious level. Because many of these beliefs are subconscious, we will work together inidentifying and bringing them to conscious awareness and then offering new ways of viewing yourself and the world. In orderto make changes in your life, it is important to understand and change these subconscious programs as well as heal and de- tach from subconscious trauma. I will also provide some tools tohelp you process trauma that is stored in cellular memory. This book is focused on helping you take ownership of your thoughts and feelings and make life-altering changes. And in order to take ownership, it is important to understand why you think and feel the way you do.

Reflection

We come into the world with a blueprint of perfection. Because we are spiritual beings entering into a material body, we already have basic information that we bring into this world. During our childhood, we begin to form belief systems about ourselves and the world and experience emotional trauma, which become the building blocks of our cognitive and emotional foundation. This becomes our story or our ego, which is a false sense of who we are. We carry these belief systems, patterns of coping and stored emotional trauma into our present and they color our experiences and influence our lives. The situations we encounter trigger emotional pain that is already there. Because many of our beliefs about ourselves and the world are not accurate, it is important for us to understand and change these belief systems as well as process unresolved emotional trauma.

Chapter 2

The Cognitive Aspect of Your Story

**The belief systems we created in childhood
influences many aspects of our lives
unless we understand and change them.**

As mentioned earlier, the belief systems based on our childhood experiences create our cognitive foundation and determineshow we view ourselves and the world. This motivates the decisions we make and influences the situations we create and attract within our lives. We carry this blueprint into our present and, until it is made conscious, addressed, and processed, it greatly impacts our lives. For example, if you grew up in an un- safe household, you may likely believe that the world is unsafe and may often times project this concept onto the world around you. You may mistrust others or feel a sense of anxiety. If you felt unloved and rejected as a child, you may likely misinterpret how other's treat you and/or primarily focus on examples of when others mistreat and reject you. You may also internalize a belief that you are not loveable or good enough, which will likely create feelings of hopelessness and sadness. If you grew up with parents who had many fears, it is highly likely you adopted those fears and they become part of the way you see the world, which can create chronic feelings of anxiety.

There are physiological reasons, which will be explored, as to why your story is so powerful and difficult to change unless you make a conscious effort to do so. However, you do not have to be the victim of your story. You have the power to rewrite your story whenever you want. You just have to believe that it is possible, fully understand it and start the process of rewriting it. Let's understand why your story is so powerful based on your physiology.

Our thoughts become habits, which is why it is so important to practice recognizing and reframing them.

First of all, your thoughts are things. They are energy. Everything is energy. You, this book, the thoughts and feelings you are experiencing as you read this. All of this is energy. Our thoughts are energy created by the brain. The brain is built of tiny nerve cells called neurons. Neurons connect to other neurons and form a neural network. When neurons connect, they create a thought, which eventually imprints in our memory. The more we think the same thought, the more we reinforce this neural connection. This is a very important concept, because this explains why it is so difficult to change how we think and, consequently, how we feel, because our thoughts are actually "hard-wired" in the brain. This also explains our attachment to our ego self. We created a story that consciously and subconscious replays itself and becomes hard wired in our brain. Think of your thoughts as habits; to break a habit takes time and intention. If you practice stopping or changing a thought, the neural connections become weaker. This book will emphasize these concepts of self-exploration and mindfulness and will provide techniques to help you change how you think. You will be encouraged to become more mindful of your conscious and subconscious thoughts and feelings and to practice consciously changing them.

Our brain subconsciously registers information that is familiar and does not fully see reality unless we change our paradigm.

In addition to your thoughts being energetically hardwired, your brain is designed to register and perceive information that fits existing paradigms created in childhood. This makes it difficult to change our beliefs about ourselves and the world as adults. When we interact with the environment, our brain assesses the information at hand, and it will only see or interpret experiences based on our past experiences. Once we have created a cognitive foundation in childhood, as an adult, it is difficult for our brain to store information that is unique because it automatically wants to categorize it into something with which it is familiar. In fact, information that does not fit what is already there is not registered. Our brain does this automatically and subconsciously before we have an opportunity to make a conscious correction. Our brain uses past information to interpret reality and canmutate it to fit these constructs. Using the previous example of feeling unloved or rejected as a child, you might misinterpretthe action of others to fit this construct. You might dismiss whensomeone does accept you and shows you love. Therefore, you are not necessarily seeing what is really there. This explains how challenging it can be to change existing belief systems, but it can be done by expanding your paradigms and creating new ways of interpreting information and being more mindful of this process.

The subconscious mind overrides the conscious mind.

In addition to how our brain processes information, it is important to understand the power of the subconscious mind. We would like to believe that we are logical, rational, and conscious thinkers. However, science has shown us that anywhere from 80-99% of all brain activity is subconscious. We can compare it to an iceberg. The tip of the iceberg is the conscious mind. The rest of the iceberg is the subconscious mind. Our subconscious mind has stored every experience we have ever had and the emotions they have elicited and registers everything. Most of our brain activity is subconscious and motivates the decisions that we make. Although we are consciously aware of a portion of our story, all of our story, even things we are not consciously aware of, is registered in the subconscious mind. This impacts how we react to and feel about our current experiences, as well as what we think and feel about ourselves and others. The subconscious mind holds more power and will override conscious thought.

For example, most of us can agree that being healthy is important but tend to engage in many unhealthy behaviors.You may have likely said "I know I need to eat healthy and exercise," which is a conscious thought, yet continue to engage in unhealthy behaviors. Because subconscious thought overrides conscious thought, these unhealthy behaviors are likely motivated by subconscious belief systems. For example, you may have a subconscious belief that you don't deserve to be healthy or that you actually want to be unhealthy because maybe that is how you received positive attention as a child. Youmight also likely have a belief system that you aren't loveable. Inthe case of weight issues, it is also possible that you felt unsafe in childhood and that you needed protection, which your body interprets as access weight. All of these beliefs combined may override the conscious idea of desiring to be healthy. If you have tired changing your diet and incorporating an exercise program, but have been unsuccessful at maintaining long term change, it may be more effective to identify and change the subconscious programs, first, which will be discussed later on. This will have more of an influence over your behavior. For example, when you realize that you deserve to be healthy or when you discover that you do not want attention for being unhealthy, you may begin to engage in healthier activities. Additionally, when you start to feel safe, your weight may change. Therefore, it is important to understand the belief systems that are stored on a subconscious level and make corrections to it. Many of the tools that will be provided focus on changing subconscious belief systems.

Our subconscious mind creates mechanisms to protect us from emotional pain.

Our brain has an inherent mechanism to distort reality as to psychologically protect us from harm so that we can survive in our environment. Because some of the experiences we encountered in childhood created emotional distress and threatened our self-esteem, psychodynamic theorists claim that our subconscious mind creates defense mechanisms as a means of coping. As children, it is difficult to psychologically accept certain realities such as we weren't safe or unconditionally loved. Whether these speculations were accurate or not, the ramification of these realizations created intense anxiety and threatened our sense of self. Our brain then adopted ways of psychologically protecting ourselves. For example, if you grew up in a violent household, this would lead you to believe that you aren't safe or loved. Experiencing constant anxiety and sadness would not be a productive way to live. Therefore, your brain would create defense mechanisms to ensure psychological survival. These defense mechanisms become part of our subconscious framework.

According to psychodynamic theory proposed by Freud, Jung, and Adler, some of the most common defense mechanisms include repression, denial, projection, displacement, sublimation, rationalization, and reaction formation. Repression is a very common defense mechanism whereby our subconscious mind prevents disturbing or threatening thoughts from entering into the conscious mind. Using the previous example of growing up in a violent household, it is advantageous to repress these memories throughout your life. Having conscious access to these memories would not be helpful. All of us, to some extent, have repressed memories from our childhoods. Denial is similar to repression. This is when we block external events from awareness and refuse to experience it. When your parents are being aggressive, for example, you may just simply deny it is happening. Projection is when we attribute our own thoughts, feelings, and motives to another person. You may get unusually angry if someone is acting like a victim, when in fact, you feel victimized and are not willing to see it. Displacement is the redirection of an impulse, usually aggression, onto a powerless substitute target. Because of your violent upbringing, this likely created anger, which may then cause you to be aggressive with others. Sublimation is similar to displacement but is a more constructive way to deal with our emotions. Creating art and journaling is a form of sublimation. Rationalization is when we cognitively distort the facts of an event to make the impulse less threatening. You may rationalize our parent's behavior by making excuses for their behavior sometimes such as blaming yourself. You may inaccurately believe that they were aggressive with you because you are bad, or you deserve it. Reaction formation is when a person goes beyond denial and behaves in the opposite way to which he or she thinks or feels. Instead of feeling anger towards your parents, you may act overly kind towards them. Although these defense mechanisms protected us from emotional pain as children and into our adult life, many of these defense mechanisms are maladaptive ways of coping with our thoughts and feelings as adults and prevent us from accessing our true subconscious belief systems and processing our emotional pain.

In addition to defense mechanisms, transactional psychologists also have explained that due to our deep existential insecurities, we create patterns of relating to others which is also learned in childhood and embedded in the subconscious mind. As mentioned earlier, we are in essence a field of energy. According to Eastern philosophy, our innate energy levels are not usually optimal. We then seek out ways in which to raise our energy levels to optimal levels. When we interact with others, we essentially merge energy fields. A dynamic inherently occurs whereby there is an opportunity for an energetic exchange. Based on learned patterns, we sometimes take from or give energy to others. We have all experienced situations when we feel either drained or uplifted based on an interaction we experienced from another person.

Because most of our parents were imperfect and innately energetically deficient, they learned to maneuver the world seeking additional energy from other people including us. Based on our parent's story, unknowingly, they engage with us through what is called control dramas, which range from passive to aggressive forms of obtaining energy. For example, a passive example of a control drama is the victim strategy, wherebythe individual seeks to gain attention and energy through the manipulation of sympathy. If a parent uses this strategy, this can cause feelings of guilt within a child and the child then gives energy as form of sympathy. The most aggressive form of control drama is intimidation, whereby the tactic of obtaining energy is through anger and hostility. If a parent uses this strategy, the child feels unsafe and drained. Depending on the control drama used by the parent and the innate temperament of the child, the child then adopts their own tactic of defending against and gaining energy. They may take a passive victim approach or a more aggressive bulling approach. Again, these patterns are learned in childhood and embedded in the subconscious mind and play out in our relationships.

In addition to creating defense mechanisms and control dramas, according to an Adlerian perspective, we also create a life script, which is sometimes conscious, but often times subconscious. Because we all feel vulnerable, innately inferior and encounter obstacles during our childhood, these scripts serve as way of coping. Birth order is one factor that influences our life script. For example, an oldest child may have a natural inclination to take care of others and feel the need to achieve. our life script. For example, an oldest child may have a natural inclination to take care of others and feel the need to achieve. may be more irresponsible. These are not necessarily absolutes because every childhood dynamic is different. Sometimes, a younger sibling may take the more responsible role if the older sibling is struggling as a way of helping out the family. These scripts are not inherently maladaptive because it is our innate feelings of inferiority that compel us to achieve great things in life. For example, a child who had a chronically sick parent, may decide to become a doctor as to resolve the anxiety of having a sick parent. However, if the unconscious motivators are not uncovered, they prevent us from accessing and correcting inaccurate beliefs and processing stored emotional pain.

Many of your beliefs are opinions, not truths and can be challenged and changed.

The belief systems that are energetically held in the subconscious mind are continually reinforced, which will likely lead you to misinterpret them as truths. I refer to these as small "t" truths. Many of the beliefs that we think are true are merely opinions, which can be changed. There are very few truths that I refer to as big "T" truths. Truths with a big "T" are universal truths such as the earth is round, the sun rises in the east and setsin the west and matter cannot be destroyed nor created only transformed. "T"ruths are absolutes, whereby everyone can agree on them. Small "t" truths are "opinions" that most of us adopt as true, usually at a very early age, because we don't challenge our belief system when we grow up. For example, the idea that "I am not lovable," "I am not good enough," etc. are a small "t" truth or opinions that we created in childhood based on our limited experiences. The concept of the "starving artist" is another small "t" truth. Some artists do financially struggle. However, some do not. Therefore, it is not a truth but an opinion.

As you start examining the beliefs that you hold, you may start to question these beliefs. Is that really true? A questionI always challenge my client's with is "Says who?" If you are holding the belief that I am not good enough, ask yourself "Says who?" You may answer, "I don't feel good enough because I never felt like I received love and approval from my father. I was always disappointing him." Ok, but does that mean you are not good enough then or now? Why is your self-worth still measured by what your father thought then or thinks now? It doesn't have to. Just because your father said or implied some judgement of you does not make it true. You could right now decide that you are good enough, despite whatever your father may or may not have said. Again, this is an opinion of your father, not a truth. We will be continuing to explore and change those small "t" truths that you hold on a subconscious level because these concepts are causing you pain and are limiting you.

We attract situations based on our subconscious beliefs.

Another reason it is so important to understand and change these subconscious constructs is because our subconscious mind is not only misinterpreting reality and not seeing everything that is truly there, but is attracting situations that support these subconscious beliefs. As mentioned before, our thoughts are energy and most of our brain power is subconscious energy. According to the law of attraction, we energetically attract circumstances that support the belief systems we hold on a conscious and more importantly subconscious level. Additionally, we subconsciously seek out situations that support our subconscious belief systems. This is based on an energetic principle that, energetically, like attracts like, which adds yet another level to how powerful the subconscious mind is. For example, you have likely noticed patterns in your life such as the people and situations you attract. You may have said, "I always seem to_____," fill in the blank; attract individuals that will abandon me, struggle with finance, etc. Again, these patterns likely stemmed from situations and beliefs that occurred in childhood. For example. If you felt like your emotional needs were not met by your mother, you will likely attract others that do not meet your emotional needs. Or ifyour family struggled with finances, you may likely find yourself in a similar situation. Therefore, to make real changes in your life, you will need to understand and change the beliefs that youhold in your subconscious mind, not just the conscious mind, detach energetically from them and create and reinforce new constructs and I will show you how.

Reflection

Although our story is powerful, it does notdefine who we are. Our thoughts become habits, which is why it is so important to practice recognizing and reframing them. Our brain subconsciously registers information that is familiar with anddoes not fully see reality unless we change our paradigms. Because our subconscious mind is more powerful than our conscious mind, it is so important to understand what is happening on a subconscious level. Our subconscious mind createsvarious coping mechanisms to protect us from emotional pain. Many of our beliefs about ourselves and the world are opinions, not Truths with a capital T andcan be challenged and changed. We attractcircumstances in our life that resonate with the conscious and more importantly subconscious beliefs that we hold.

Chapter 3

The Emotional Aspect of Your Story

Unprocessed emotional experiences are stored in your cellular memory and can be cleared.

Now that you understand your cognitive foundation, let's explore the emotions that are attached to the story that you are rewriting. As mentioned earlier, as infants, we expressed emotions without restraints. As we grew up, we experienced situations that created feelings we likely suppressed. We store these unexpressedand unprocessed emotions in our physical energy field within our body. They affect our daily life and will manifest themselves sooner or later because how we consciously and subconsciously appraise current reality triggers these unprocessed emotions. It is also highly likely that these unprocessed emotions will surface even if not necessarily triggered possibly manifesting as sadness, anxiety, or physical ailments. Therefore, it is important for you to explore and process the emotional experiences that are stored within your cellular memory.

We all have endured trauma on some level. Although most of us did not necessarily encounter devastating traumas suchas wars, attacks, sexual assaults, etc., which I refer to as big"T" traumas. We all have encountered little "t" traumas suchas being criticized by a parent, not receiving love and approval from a sibling and other hurtful and scary experiences fromour childhood. These traumas are just as impactful as big "T" traumas and affect our day-to-day life. Yet, as adults we tend to minimize the emotions we endured in our childhood.

One of the reasons we have emotions is to imprint events into our memory. This mechanism is paramount to our survival. As a child, if you attempted to place your hand on the stoveand your mother yelled at you, for example, you would have been flooded with emotions. This would assist in solidifying this memory. Although in time this memory would likely be hidden from your conscious mind, unless you severely burned yourself, the subconscious memory would assist you in remembering that you should be careful around stoves. Although this mechanism is helpful in some cases, it is not advantageous if, for example, your mother was yelling at you about a lot of different things which were not necessarily important.

Our brain's information processing system has a natural tendency to process trauma so that it is no longer painful, but this system can be blocked by unprocessed trauma. It is speculated that it is during REM sleep that we process memories. You can compare your brain to a computer. As mentioned in the previous chapter, when information comes in, our brain needs to file it somewhere. It files it based on constructs already created. However, significant trauma, such as an attack, because this may be unfamiliar, the brain does not know where to store it. Because it is heavily encoded with emotional content, the brain also has difficulty discarding it. It then is not properly stored, which creates, so to speak, a glitch in the system, which is why individuals with severe trauma experience flashbacks, nightmares, and other posttraumatic stress symptoms.

There is another type of prolonged trauma that creates a similar glitch in our brain's processing system. For example, if your father yelled at you once in a while, during REM sleep, you probably were able to process this small "t" trauma. However, if he yelled at you quite often and there was a lot of conflict happening at home, there might be too much content for your brain to process during REM sleep. These unprocessed memories would cause a similar glitch in the brain's processing system. These repeated situations can also create a conditioned response. You are probably familiar with Pavlov and his experiments with dogs. We similarly become conditioned. Taste aversion is an example of an affective conditioning method. If you became violently ill after eating tuna fish, for example, you will likely never be able to eat tuna fish again or at least for quite a while. If during your childhood, your father was yelling at you quite often, it is highly likely you would have a conscious or subconscious emotional response to future authority figures. The good news is whatever the trauma, there are techniques to help the brain process this information that will be described later.

You are probably not fully aware that you have trauma and emotional pain that is physically stored within your body. As you read through this book and begin working on self-exploration, it will be important for you to truly connect to the feelings you experienced as a child and not minimize them. It is important to understand just how emotionally impactful your experiences were as a child. Research has shown that infants, even when given sustenance such as food and water, will not survive if not given love and nurturing. This is why painful childhood experiences are so deeply encoded within our body. No matter how trivial they may seem to us as adults, these emotional conflicts were incredibly painful for us as children, because they were so important to our survival. For example, if we were criticized or ignored by a parent, we may react with intense emotions such as sadness and fear because to an infant, not receiving love meant possible death. Additionally, some of our trauma may have occurred as early as prenatally. It is important to have as much information as possible about your early childhood circumstances, which you can reference as we proceed further into self-exploration.

Conscious and subconscious negative emotions disrupt your energetic and biochemical system.

Our body not only has a biochemical makeup but an energetic one which needs to be in balance if it is to function correctly. Our energetic system is the precursor to biochemical reactions. This concept is not emphasized in our western culture but is the foundation of eastern medicine. Whether we are conscious of it or not, when present situations trigger unprocessed and unresolved emotions, it creates emotional pain that disrupts the energetic system, which then triggers a biochemical reaction.

Our body is wise. Our cells, organs, nerves, and muscles know how to innately communicate. However, on our journey in the material world, we encounter several influences that disrupt this flow of information. We experience emotional and physical stress. We also encounter toxins, nutritional deficiencies, electromagnetic frequencies (EMFs), pathogens etc. that disrupt the communication within our physical bodies. All of these factors, disrupt the flow of information within our body and are the antecedents for both physical and emotional illnesses. Our unresolved feelings and continually triggered emotional scars are not only the contributors to emotional illnesses such as depression and anxiety but also impact our physical wellbeing because they disrupt our energetic and biochemical systems. Therefore, it is important to get in touch and fully process these emotions that are trapped within our energetic bodies.

We become addicted to emotions we regularly experience, and this damages the body.

When we interact with our environment, our brain subconsciously assesses the information at hand. We then have an emotional response to the situation at that moment. These chemicalsare created in the hypothalamus located in the brain. The brain creates a chemical that matches every emotion that we experience. When we feel an emotion, the brain assembles the appropriate chemical and then releases it into the bloodstream. There is a chemical for every emotion, such as anger, fear, and sadness. Every cell in your body has thousands of receptor sites for all of our emotions, and these chemicals attach to these receptor sites, which activates the cell and alters it. Each cell is alive and possesses consciousness, and it craves these chemical reactions. When we experience an emotion on a regular basis, our cell creates more receptor sites for that chemical, similar to how our cells change when we use of psychotropic drugs. If we become sad or angry every day, our cells will eventually crave sadness or anger. We then actually become addicted to those emotional experiences, similar to as to how we get addicted to our thought processes.

Because our cells are impacted by emotional experiences, intense emotional experiences can damage cells if they create an abundance of receptor sites that do not allow other important things to enter the cell, such as nutrients. This compromises our health and ages us, which is why dealing with your emotions is not only vital for emotional wellbeing, but physical health as well. You can't separate the mind from the body because they work synergistically. Indeed, more and more researchers are speculating that a lot, if not most, of our illnesses are rooted in our emotional experiences, especially childhood trauma. This is why healing emotional scars is so important. We cannot sustain good health if we are continually experiencing negative emotions on a daily basis.

Chronic emotional distress activates the flight or fight response and dysregulates the endocrine system.

Stressors such as emotional trauma activates a series of complex nervous and biochemical communications that prepare the body's nervous, hormonal, and immune systems to respond to impending or potential threats known as the flight or fight response. Here is how this mechanism works. Information from our environment is first registered by our senses via the brain stem and relayed to a portion of our brain known as the limbic system, which contains left and right temporal lobes or amygdala. If the amygdala determines that this new information is a threat, by comparing this to stored memories, it sounds an alarm and sends a report to the orbitofrontal cortex and then to the hypothalamus, which is the link to the nervous systems to the endocrine system via the pituitary. It first sends a message to the adrenals to stimulate the production of adrenaline which activates the sympathetic nervous system and creates physiological responses such as increased heart rate, muscle tension, etc. to prepare the body to fight or flee the situation. Then it signals the pituitary gland to produce Adrenocorticotropic hormone ACTH, which stimulates the adrenal cortex to produce cortisol. Cortisol activates the parasympathetic nervous system resulting in increased blood sugar and suppressed immune and digestive systems, which counterbalances the sympathetic fight or flight system to ensure that these systems do not become overstressed.

Although this system is advantageous when there is an actual physical threat, this mechanism turns on when there is a perceived emotional threat. When we experience chronic stress, this fight or flight responses is continuously triggered and dysregulation will eventually occur within the endocrine system, primarily the hypothalamus, pituitary, and adrenal systems. For example, if you grew up in an environment where your parents yelled often, when you would encounter yelling, this system is likely triggered. This becomes compounded and causes chronic dysregulation within the endocrine system and eventually the body starts to break down. Therefore, when we encounter a situation that resembles the original trauma, this will subconsciously trigger these sympathetic and parasympathetic responses.

Chronic emotional distress also creates chronic inflammation and depresses the immune system.

In addition to the endocrine system, the lymphatic and immune systems play a role in the fight or flight response. Because we are not always able to fully process our emotions, it is speculated that unprocessed emotions start to collect in the lymph system just like physical toxins. When there is an excess of stress, the lymphatic system generates a reaction such as a fever to help release these emotional toxins from the body. Lymphatic reactions may actually help us process stressful emotional events so that we can let go and move on. The lymph system is made of several hundred lymph nodes. As lymph moves through the body, it absorbs and helps remove toxins, bacteria, digested fats, hormones, and other waste products. It produces and stores white blood cells including t-cells that are responsible for destroying life-threatening pathogens. Your fighter B and T lymphocytes function in part by forming memories of specific pathogens. The immune system has a hard time distinguishing between those life-threatening pathogens and other new invaders that look similar. Using the example of chronic yelling in the house, the lymph system reacts to emotional threats that may resemble the original trauma, which leads to inflammation and suppressed immune system. This is just part of the physiological responses that occur from chronic emotional stress, illustrating just how important it is to process not only conscious emotional responses, but subconscious ones as well.

Our DNA contains cellular memory from our parents, ancestors, and past lives.

Theorists speculate that our DNA contains cellular memory from our ancestors, parents, and our past lives that adds yet another dimension to our story because these memories reinforce our belief systems and compound our emotional experiences. As mentioned previously, our emotions are there to imprint experiences into memory as a way of learning. Traumas are coupled with intense emotional experiences and encoded in our brain and then passed down to generations to protect the lineage. For example, researchers have exposed rats to phobias that become apparent generations later. Researchers have also subjected rats to famine and the generations later the rats showed signs of obesity, as a result of an inborn fear of hunger. Based on this research, it is speculated that this also occurs in humans. Although this may have served a purpose in earlier years, this mechanism is no longer relevant or helpful. For example, famine is no longer a concern as it was for our ancestors. Therefore, it is no longer advantageous to hold the memories that may trigger our metabolism or behaviors to hold onto weight. If we had a lineage of financial scarcity, the fear of being poor, for example, is not helpful if we have access to resources. Keeping in mind the law of attraction, subconscious concepts of scarcity, whether it be resources, love, money, or opportunities will only make those things more difficult to attract in our lives.

In addition to ancestral lineage, our parent's experiences heavily impact us subconsciously and can create conflicts and repeated patterns. It would be logical to assume that their beliefs, patterns, and traumas are even more impactful than ancestral information. If we are not mindful, we can even replay patterns in our lives. Sometimes, we get married or have children the same time they did. We may develop illnesses or have a serious accident around the same ages as a parent did. According to Esogetic Colorpuncture theory, which is rooted in Traditional Chinese Medicine, we also physically imprint information. For ex-ample, we imprint information from our father on our throats and lower back. If our father was conflicted, we may have difficulty speaking our truth or standing up for ourselves, so to speak. We imprint information from our mothers on our navel and back of the neck, which may manifest in digestive issues or neck pain.

29

Christina Samycia, PsyD

The good news is, you can stop these dysfunctional patterns by understanding them and processing them. Even more profound is by processing the traumas from your ancestors and parents, not only are you helping yourself, but you are also in essence helping the next generation and healing previous generations.

Many spiritual teachings subscribe to the concept of reincarnation. Because we are eternal spiritual beings, the material body we are inhabiting right now is only one of many. If we are eternal, it would only make sense that we experience many different lifetimes. Many of these experiences, especially the painful and emotionally charged ones, also become encoded in our DNA. Whether it is true reincarnation that we are really inhabiting other bodies, or just memories of ancestral memories stored in our DNA, it may not really matter. The importantconcept to understand is that we come in this lifetime withpreprogrammed data that is stored in our genetic material, such as emotional memories of death, love, loss and so many different human experiences. This emotional memory as wellas belief systems that were learned in these lifetimes become part of our subconscious process that influences our lives. For example, some of our phobias are rooted in past lives. If you drowned in a past life, you might have a fear of water, which canbe processed through techniques such as regression hypnosis. If there was something unresolved in a past life, such as you weren't able to rescue your child from harm, you might have an unhealthy feeling of being overly responsible for that person in your present life which may have returned as a parent. If thereis a karmic pattern of betrayal by loved ones, you may have anxiety and paranoia in your present life. All of these patterns can be cleared by utilizing the techniques that will be explored later on.

The emotional pain from these traumas along with the belief systems that were created because of them, also impact our daily life even if these experiences never actually happened to us because they are physically registered in the body. This is why some of our belief systems and emotional pain does not always make sense. Some of us have phobias we don't understand, attachments to people and concepts and feelings of familiarity to certain situations, places and ideas that are just not logical. Therefore, it is important to understand that these memories and the belief systems created serve to amplify the emotional experiences we have from this lifetime.

As you continue on your journey of self-exploration, youmight find it helpful to understand the other stores that are part of your subconscious program. It is important to understand the full picture before we move to the next step of clearing these beliefs and the emotions attached to them, because some of these traumatic memories influence us in a deep way and add toour suffering. Sometimes, they are just as impactful as traumasthat have actually occurred to us in the present day.

There are other sources of our emotional distress.

In addition to unresolved emotional material that remains unprocessed in cellular memory, there are other factors that can trigger emotions such as sadness and anxiety. Just like the body creates pain to alert us that something is wrong physically, our emotions can also be an indication that there is problem in our life. Sometimes, our intuition is registering something in the environment and is creating an emotional response to alert us to a situation that might be potentially harmful or dangerous. If you are experiencing dread about going to work, for example, it may be that something in your work environment, such as the people, environment or other unhealthy dynamics are present. Your dread may also be an indication that this job or the work you are doing is no longer right for you. Or if you are in a relationship with a person that is harmful to you, you may begin to experience unexplained sadness.

There is a small population of individuals referred to as empaths, who actually feel the emotions of others. Because of this, empaths may experience emotions that are not necessarily theirs. Not only do empaths feel the emotions of others, but they can even feel physical pain of others. Empaths are also usually highly sensitive. They can be over stimulated by bright lights, loud noises, crowds and environmental chemicals, which may trigger an emotional response. Some of the tools illustrated later on can be useful to help process these emotions.

When we are not following our spiritual or life path, the conflict between the ego and spiritual self can also create feelingsof despair and anxiety. Because we come into this lifetimewith information as to what we are to learn, accomplish and experience, our subconscious alerts us when we are deviating from this path.

Hormone and neurotransmitter disruption can also be exacerbating our emotions. Our emotions can also be impacted by a disruption in our gut health, pathogens including heavy metals, parasites, bacteria, and viruses, as well as other physical imbalances. Nutritional deficiencies can also impact how we feel. These are some things to keep in mind as we start the process of self-discovery because it is wise to get clarity on the sources of your distress.

Reflection

Unprocessed emotional trauma is registered within our body's energeticframework and is continually triggered. This creates dysregulation within the bodyand contributes to emotional and physical ailments. However, this can be remedied. We have all encountered trauma from our childhood registered within our cellular memory. Other sources, including cellularmemories of traumas from our parents, ancestors and past lives can influence ourcurrent emotional state. Additionally, our subconscious mind may send us signalsthat something is wrong in our lives, whichcan elicit an emotional response.

Chapter 4

Exploring and Understanding Your Story

It is helpful to create a narrative of your story.

The first step along your journey of discovering inner peace is to start exploring and understanding your story. This will help clarify the belief systems you have created, how you are appraising your current reality, and the emotional pain that is triggered. Now that you understand the foundation of your suffering, your work begins. As you have discovered, the two main components of your suffering are inaccurate belief systems, both conscious and subconscious, that trigger emotional responses and unresolved emotional trauma that is stored in your cellular memory. You are now aware that many of your stress-provoking beliefs about yourself and the world are not true because these beliefs were created in childhood with your child-like lenses and limited life experiences. Therefore, many of your beliefs are opinions, not truths and can be challenged and changed. Before you can start rewriting your story, it is important to start exploring your story and identifying belief systems that are no longer serving you on a conscious and subconscious level, as well as identifying the emotional pain they trigger.

Starting a journal is an excellent way to accomplish this. You can begin the journaling process by writing the narrative of your story to discover the conscious and subconscious beliefs that you are carrying, as well as any emotional trauma that may be stored in your cellular memory. It is important that you write out this narrative and all future journaling rather than type it because hand writing provides you with better access to subconscious material. Handwriting your journaling can also be cathartic, which is quite beneficial. When drafting your narrative, it is valuable to start this story prenatally, if possible. When you begin your narrative, start with the beginning of your story, the time between conception and birth. Here are some questions you may want to answer to help you fill in all the details of your story.

• What situation where you born into? What wereyour parent's and family member's experiences during your conception, prenatal stage, and birth?

• Were there any unusual circumstances that happened around your conception, prenatal stage and/or at birth? Did you have any trauma at birth?

• Were there any significant events that occurred after you were born?

• How did your parents relate to you?

• Did you have siblings? If so, what was their experience during your prenatal stage and around your birth?

After you gather information regarding your history from conception to birth, start writing about your childhood.

• Who were your primary caregivers? What was your relationship with your primary caregivers? What was your relationship with your parents?

• What was your relationship with your siblings? What was the dynamic with them? How did you feel about them? How did they feel about you?

• How did you view yourself as a child? What was your role in the family?

• How would you describe the members in your immediate family? Extended family?

Christina Samycia, PsyD

- What are some major events that transpired during your childhood?
- If you went to daycare, what was your experience? What was your relationship with your babysitters, nannies, and other care givers if you had any?
- What experiences did you have in school? During the summer?
- What were your relationships with your friends and peers?
- What were the causes of stress in your household?
- What caused you stress during your childhood?
- How did you feel about school, social activities, etc.?
- What are some memories that stand out to you?

Now start gathering information regarding your life after you grew up.

- What experiences did you have?
- What relationships did you have?
- Where did you go to school? What did you study?
- What jobs did you have?
- What are some significant life events that transpired in your adult life?

All of these questions can lead you to a better understanding of the details of your story. In addition to your story, it is also helpful to gather information regarding your parent's storiesand even grandparent's stories. Now that you have gathered information regarding your story and the stories of your parent's and ancestors, you will begin uncovering your conscious and subconscious belief systems as well as any emotional trauma that may be stored in your cellular memory. Here are some examples. If you had a birth trauma, this could explain chronic anxiety. Maybe your mother felt conflicted about having a child. This could create a belief system of not feeling wanted, which could lead to chronic feelings of sadness. Maybe your birth created anxiety within the family due to financial strain. This may create a belief system of feeling overly responsibility for situations and guilt. Maybe your siblings did not welcome a new child. This could create a belief of not being loveable and feelings of sadness and abandonment. When you start writing out a narrative, you will likely start to notice patterns. These patterns will lead you to beliefs that may be stored on a subconscious level. Take some time to examine this narrative and start to identify the beliefs about yourself and the world that were created because of this story and the emotions these experiences elicited so that you can now start challenging and changing them.

You may also want to keep a journal of daily stressors.

After you have journaled the narrative of your story and started identifying some belief systems that you would like to change and some unprocessed emotional trauma you would like to clear,you can also choose to keep a daily journal to continue assistingyou further in uncovering subconscious beliefs and unprocessed emotional material. You may choose to start your journaling by exploring situations that are creating distress in your life now and identify how you might appraise them based on your story and the subconscious belief systems that are triggering emotional responses. It may be helpful to take some time to write down the circumstances in your life that are creating distress as well as identifying the emotions that they are triggering. Once you have written several situations down, examine the one that is creating the most distress. Become clear about your thoughts and feelings regarding this situation and start writing them down without judging or minimizing them. Now, based on your childhood experiences, determine where these thoughts and feelings came from. Ask yourself the following questions: "How am I viewing this situation?" "What feeling is this situation triggering? Why?" "Where did I feel this before," "Why am I perceiving the situation the way I do," and "Based on what I learned about my story, what are some belief systems that I hold that are resonating with this situation?"

Here are some examples that may be helpful. Let's say you notice in your journal that you become irrationally upset, anxious and sad when things are not going perfectly in your life. You may realize that your constant striving for perfection is causing you stress. When you ask yourself why is being perfect important, you realize that you created a belief system in childhood that you needed to be perfect to receive love because you never felt as though you could please your parents. Therefore, a belief you may choose to work on is "I am not lovable or good enough" and the emotion you may choose to process is sadness.

In another example, you may also notice that you become unreasonably upset when your partner is not listening to you. You may ask yourself, "Why is this upsetting me so much?" You may remember that there was significant chaos in your family, and you often felt invisible, which triggers feelings of abandonment and anxiety and created a belief that "I don't matter" and "I'm not important".

Or in another example, you may find that you are struggling with your boss, who is authoritarian and demanding. You notice that you react and become distraught any time he would offer constructive criticism. You are reminded that this resembles the dynamic with your own hard-to-please authoritative father. This situation elicits feelings of sorrow and inadequacy, as it dredges up your old emotions of your father.

It is important to link your past emotional experiences and the belief systems that contribute to this distress. Then repeat the process with the other situations you wrote down. Practice linking the past to the present to understand why you think and feel the way you do. Use the narrative you created as a reference for your further journaling. You can now start the process of change by understanding how and why you think and feel the way you do. Now that you are becoming more conscious of your thoughts and feelings, you can start the process of relating them back to their origins. By re-examining your past, you can see how it has shaped your present. Therefore, it is important to find that link to the past that explains why you feel and think the way that you do now; this is the key to better understand your full story.

Journaling about childhood memories may be helpful.

As you continue journaling, it may be helpful to also explore any childhood memories that trigger negative emotions. These memories are the keys to unlocking themes that may create emotional pain as well as unprocessed emotions. In the next few sections, you will learn some techniques to help process some of the emotional pain from these memories. As mentioned earlier, during this process, ask yourself the following questions: How did these childlike experiences mold my emotional experiences? How did these experiences shape how I see myself and the world? What belief systems did I create because of some of these experiences? As you start to recall these memories, imagine yourself as a child reliving these experiences to really identify how you felt without minimizing or denying the feelings.

Patterns are clues to subconscious belief systems.

As you continue journaling for a while, you will also start to notice patterns. For example, are you attracting similar circumstances or people into your life? Are you noticing that you often struggle with the same issues such as finances, relationships, work, health, etc.? Do you notice recurring feelings of depression, anxiety, or anger? These patterns are clues to subconscious belief systems that you likely hold. Again, some of these belief systems may not be logical or rational based on your current life experiences because they may have been created by a parent, ancestor, or a past life.

Christina Samycia, PsyD

Patterns in relationships are especially helpful to understand what is occurring subconsciously. Understanding the feelings that result from the dynamics in your relationships can also lead you to understand your scars from the past because we often chose relationships with others to resolve past psychological conflicts. We tend to pick significant others, friends, coworkers, and acquaintances that resemble our parents, siblings, or other significant individuals from our past, which can reflect our unresolved unconscious desires and needs. Although most of us understand that relationships with our parents play a role in future relationships, other significant relationships, such as siblings, are just as influential. We are attracted to others because the dynamic feels familiar. Moreover, we want to emotionally "fix" the things we were unable to fix in our past. Because we didnot satisfy an emotional need that was established in our earlier years, we try to get it from the people in our present life, but this only leaves us frustrated, hurt, and disappointed when it invariably is not met. We also find it difficult to leave these dysfunctional relationships, because we have this psychological need that has not been met. This dynamic may prevent us from having healthy relationships.

For example, if you felt rejected by a parent, you will likely seek out individuals similar to that parent who will likely reject you. You may tend to continue to stay in these relationships hoping that you will finally get the love and validation that you have been seeking. Or if you had a younger sibling that was always needing help, you might likely seek out a relationship where you find yourself constantly helping that person. Although this may make you frustrated, you will likely continue this dynamic because it is familiar and that there is a subconscious wish to fix this person. It is also highly likely that you built your self-esteem around being the more responsible sibling that was always there to help, which may also keep you trapped in this dynamic.

What patterns are you uncovering in your current relationships? How are they linked to your childhood relationships with your mother, father, siblings, and other significant relationships from childhood? What belief systems are playing out through these dynamics? What emotional pain are they triggering?

Reflection

To fully understand your story, begin journaling a narrative and start identifying some belief systems that you would like to change and some unprocessed emotional trauma you would like to clear. You can also choose to keep a daily journal of stressors to continue assisting you further in uncovering subconscious beliefs and unprocessed emotional material. As you identify current stressors, you may want to link the past with the present to understand why you think and feel the way you do.

Chapter 5

Additional Things to Keep in Mind

Observe, not judge, or minimize your past.

One of the things to keep in mind is that when you begin examining your past, as well as how you think, feel, and behave, it is important that you observe, not judge it. Being judgmental about how you think, feel, and act or have acted is not productive. Your job is to be the observer, not to be critical of what happened, how you reacted or of how you think and feel about it. It is also important that you observe your past without minimizing it. When you examine your past, you may think "It wasn't that bad," or "It's understandable why things happened the way they did," or "My parents treated me the way they did because of the circumstances that they were having." You may also think, "It's in the past, and there is nothing I can do about it." However, to really understand what is occurring on a subconscious level and to truly process it, it is important to not minimize or rationalize the events that happened. It is important to get in touch with how you actually felt as a child during this experience.

Having and feeling emotions
does not make you weak.

When embarking on self-exploration, this likely brings up feelings of sadness, anger, anxiety, etc., but these emotions are perfectly normal and healthy. When you are honest with how you think and feel, you may feel vulnerable, which is not to be confused with weakness. However, some people believe that feeling emotions makes them "weak," which can be an obstacle in self-exploration. One of the reasons that we think expressing emotions is a sign of weakness is that we don't fully understand them, which is why our emotions have sometimes been painful in the past.

Emotions are part of who we are, and it is important to feel comfortable feeling and expressing them. We might also have seen others displaying emotions inappropriately and perceive them as being unstable. However, it is important to remember that feeling your emotions is not necessarily being overwhelmed by your emotions, and even if you are, this is ok. By avoiding your emotions, by stuffing them inside because you are afraid of them, is not much different from an overly emotional display. It is just the opposite end of the same spectrum. These emotions will eventually surface sooner or later. Even if you attempt to avoid them, they are still being triggered and impacting you in a negative way. It takes a strong person to be able to go back and look at the past and one's self honestly. We all feel hurt, sad, scared, disappointed, and vulnerable and just because we have these feelings does not mean we are not strong and secure. Having feelings is a natural part of being human. Therefore, the healthiest and strongest place is to feel and express your emotions in a healthy way. In future sections, we will explore techniques on how to process these emotions in a healthy way.

Everyone experiences emotional pain.

Another obstacle to self-exploration is that you may fear that if you explored your emotions, you might find something wrong with you. Our lack of knowledge about our emotional lives prevents some of us from self-reflection. However, everyone experiences emotional pain. Everyone at some point in their lives feels sad, anxious, angry, frustrated, lonely, etc. This is part of the human experience. Because our emotional self is so personal to us, it is highly vulnerable to scrutiny. The idea that "I am not feeling okay" has, in some ways, been misconstrued to mean, "I am not okay." This is because it is difficult to separate our feelings from who we are, but it is important to realize you are not your feelings. Your feelings are just a part of who you are. There does not have to be a stigma attached to having and exploring these feelings. I find it interesting that, in our society, we do not have a problem going to a doctor if we have a physical ailment, but we feel that we need to struggle alone with our emotional needs. It may be that we do not view our physical health as personally, but having a physical ailment is not any different than feeling depressed or anxious. It could be that physical ailments are viewed differently from psychological ailments because we are not taught to believe that everyone suffers and that our emotions are biochemical reactions. Furthermore, many of our physical ailments are routed in emotional trauma. Therefore, it isimportant to put our emotional wellbeing in perspective and dealwith it just as we would deal with any physical ailment.

Your childhood experiences
do not define who you are.

Additionally, we fear that the discovery of a dysfunctional childhood would reflect poorly upon us. Some of us feel ashamed of our childhood experiences. However, you are not the sum of your experiences. Everyone has a dysfunctional childhood to some degree. When we were children, we were, to some extent, victims of our situation because we were unable to make the choices that we can make as adults. We also did not yet have the tools we needed to cope with these situations. But at any moment, you can choose not to continue being the victim of your past and change how you think, feel, and act once you understand the process. Your past does not have to define who you are in the present. You are who you choose to be in the present and you can decide who you want to be in the future.

Christina Samycia, PsyD

We have all been scarred by the past. This is what we all share. Our past creates emotional scars, and personal growth is the process of uncovering and healing those scars. This is nothing to ever feel ashamed of, no matter what has happened to you.

Common inaccurate belief systems
that most of us share.

Now that you have examined some obstacles to self-exploration, as you continue with your journaling, you will start to identify some belief systems that you created that are triggering emotional pain. Here are some fairly common beliefs that most of us struggle with:

- I am not good enough.
- I am not loveable.
- I don't deserve to be happy or to get what I want.
- I am all alone.
- I don't belong.
- I am not safe.
- I can't trust anyone.
- People are always hurting me, treating poorly, etc.
- I can't create the life I want.
- Money, love, [whatever you desire] is hard to get or keep.

Remember, these beliefs are opinions, not truths and can be changed at any time. These beliefs are triggering emotional pain and are hurting you. They are keeping you from finding inner peace and the life that you want and deserve. Now, that you have explored your story and started identifying some belief sys-tems that you hold as well as identifying the emotional pain that they trigger, it is time to look at some new paradigms to start challenging and changing these beliefs that are ultimately harm-ing and limiting you.

Reflection

To fully get in touch with subconscious emotions, it is important to observe not judge your past and understand that having and feeling your emotions is perfectly normal and healthy. It is part of being human. Your childhood experiences do not define who you are. Some of the common inaccurate belief systems that most of us share include: I am not good enough, I am not loveable, I don't deserve to be happy or to get what I want, etc., I am all alone, I don't belong, I am not safe, I can't trust anyone, People are always hurting me, treating poorly, etc., I can't create the life I want and Money, love, etc. is hard to get, keep, etc. These beliefs are opinions, not truths and can be changed at any time.

Part 2

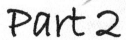

Rewriting Your Story

New paradigms
to help you change your belief

systems

"Life isn't about finding yourself.
Life is about creating yourself."
—George Bernard Shaw

Introduction to Part 2

You Have the Power to Rewrite Your Story

Hopefully, you have started journaling a narrative and have identified the circumstances in your life that are causing you distress. Based on this information, you have now identified belief systems that no longer serve you and the dysfunctional emotions they elicit. You are now ready to begin making some paradigm shifts. Are you ready to make some profound changes in your life? Are you ready to let go of these beliefs that are trapping you in suffering and limiting you? Are you ready to let go of sadness, anxiety, fear, anger and all those emotions that cause you pain? Great! Now, you can start rewriting your story by creating new belief systems on a conscious level. Once you do that, you can begin healing emotional trauma from cellular memory and detaching energetically from these belief systems that are triggering pain on a subconscious level, which will be addressed in Part 3. You have the ability to change and rewrite your story so let's continue!

"It doesn't matter how long we've had negative patterns. The point of power is always in the present moment. This is where the change takes place right here right now."

—Louise Hay

Chapter 6

You Are Powerful

Understanding that you are powerful is one of the most important paradigm shifts.

One common belief system that creates feelings of sadness, anxiety or hopelessness and keeps us trapped in dysfunctional patterns is believing that you are a victim in your life. Although we are raised believing that the world is bigger and more powerful than we are, a major paradigm shift is to start embracing just how powerful you truly are. Moving from being a victim to the creator of your life is probably the most important paradigmshift, because it is the foundation of the other paradigms to be discussed. Keep in mind, you choose to come here to fulfill a unique destiny and have amazing gifts to offer. You are part of a bigger picture and have exciting lessons to learn. You are wise, powerful, resilient, and amazing!

You always have a choice in how you perceive and respond to situations in your life.

You are powerful for so many reasons. One way in which you are powerful is that although you may not always have control over all the circumstances in your life, you always have the ability to change how you think, feel, and respond to them. Nothing has power over you because nothing has the ability to make you think and feel a certain way. You always have a choice. However, often, your thoughts and feelings appear to happen automatically, because much of how you are thinking and feeling about your circumstance is happening on a subconscious level. You do not always realize that you have time to understand how you are appraising these situations and then decide how to reframe and respond to them. With practice, you can learn to stop, pause, and access before engaging in a response. When you are in a situation that triggers a negative emotion such as sadness, anger, anxiety, you have the opportunity to pause, then take a deep breath and then ask yourself the following questions: Why am I feeling this way? What is this situation triggering in me? How am I viewing this situation and why? How can I look atthis in a different way?

Here is an example to illustrate this. Let's say you notice that you become stressed when you attempt to do something, such as create a presentation for work, and it does not turn out as well as you would have wanted. When you examine this, you realized that you feel stressed, sad, and anxious when you believe that things aren't going perfectly. After looking at your thoughts, try to understand where they originated. Then stop, pause, and ask yourself: What emotional scar is this situation triggering? In this case, it might be that you inaccurately believe that in order to receive approval from others, you need to be perfect. Your unhappiness may have been created because you did not feel as though you received approval from your parents. Striving for perfection is exhausting. You can believe that you are ok even if you are not perfect and that you are no longer the little child that desires approval.

It is helpful to start taking ownership over your thoughts and feelings through self-examination and awareness. Understanding conscious and subconscious dynamics, will empower you as you begin to understand why you think and feel the way youdo. When you become more aware of your emotional life by understanding it and bringing it to consciousness, this will start to give you the ability to change your perceptions and reactions and ultimately feel more empowered. You have an opportunity right now to take charge of your life. When something happens and you feel sad, disappointed, hurt, or anxious, you can choose to believe that you are powerful and understand why you think and feel the way you do and feel something different. You have control over your thoughts and emotions, and by understanding them and wanting to change, you no longer have to believe that you are a victim in your life. Additionally, you will be learning techniques that will lessen the energetic charge surrounding situations that trigger emotional responses which will also help you feel more empowered. Utilizing the techniques that I will provide in the next section; you will likely notice that situations that once triggered you will likely lessen or possibly not trigger you at all.

You are not the victim of your reality, but the creator of it.

Earlier I stated that we may not always have control over all the circumstances in our lives; however, I do believe that we contribute to some, if not most of the circumstances that we attract into our life. We definitely are co-creators of our reality, which is the second example of how powerful you are. Louise Hay states in her book Power Is Within You, a resource I highly recommend along with her books Heal Your Body and You Can Heal Your Life, "We contribute toward the creation of every condition in our lives, good or bad, with our thinking, feeling patterns. The thoughts we think create our feelings, and we then begin to live our lives in accordance with those feelings and beliefs. This is not to blame ourselves for things going wrong in our lives. There is a difference between being responsible and blaming ourselves or others…Blame is about giving away one's power. Responsibility gives us the power to make changes in our lives. Responsibility is our ability to respond to a situation… By taking responsibility, we have the power to change. We can say, 'What can I do to make this different?'" Therefore, if you are in a situation that is undesirable, instead of taking the victim position and asking, "Why is this happening to me?" it is more empowering to ask, "What subconscious programs do I have that attracts this dynamic to me?" or "What am I supposed to learn from this situation?"

As mentioned previously, we attract some circumstances in our lives based on our subconscious and conscious belief systems. We also attract situations because there is a life lesson we need to learn through this experience, which will be elaborated on in future sections. There is a basic metaphysical principle referred to as the law of attraction. Our thoughts and feelings are energy. Like energy attracts like. The thoughts we focus on consciously and more importantly subconsciously attract similar experiences into our lives. Science has shown us very interesting evidence that suggests just how powerful we are. According to quantum physics, all matter exists in a wave of possibilities. It is only when the observer, the "I," fixates on a point that it materializes. Therefore, without the observer, even material objects would not exist as we know it. It is only when we perceive something that it actually begins to exist in reality. This has profound implications of how powerful we are. This perspective can help you shift from victim to creator of your life.

When we want to change the circumstances in our lives, most of us tend to look at what we can change externally. However, a more effective way of changing your circumstances is to change your conscious, and more importantly, subconscious beliefs. When you change your thinking, your external reality changes. For example, if you find yourself struggling with finances, before focusing on finding a better job, or starting a budget, it's more advantageous to first understand and shift your belief systems about money. If you believe that money is evil, or that money is difficult to obtain, this prevents you from attracting and/or holding onto money. Once you shift your beliefs, your behaviors will change and the situations you attract in your life will as well. Therefore, it is important to make a shift from being the victim to taking responsibility for the reality that you are creating. By making changes in how you think and the beliefs you hold on a conscious and subconscious level, you can create a different reality. You will start attracting and manifesting new situations. "There is a power within each of us that can lovingly direct us to perfect health, perfect relationships and perfect careers. First, we have to believe that it is possible. Next, we must be willing to release the patterns in our lives that are creating conditions that we don't want," Louise Hay.

Because the universe mirrors for us what we believe on a conscious and more importantly subconscious level, it is so important to become aware of these subconscious programs and start to change them as well as becoming more mindful of the things we say and think and even the messages we expose ourselves to because this can reinforce belief systems we want to shift. Start paying attention to the things you say outloud and to yourself and start the practice of reframing them. Keep in mind, the subconscious mind is very powerful. It hears everything. What are the things you say to yourself or out loud on a regular basis? What messages are you exposed to on a daily basis? Are they fear-based or negative? This impacts your reality. This can be difficult to avoid because there are so many fear-based messages that we are exposed to on a regularbasis. However, when you start becoming more mindful, you willlikely start noticing how frequently we are bombarded by fear- based messages. Hopefully, you will become more mindful of the information that you allow into your life.

For example, watching the news is very anxiety provoking and reinforces our fears. The media reinforces that idea that theworld isn't safe by reporting crimes, terrorism, and other atrocities.

Additionally, our medical community is not promoting "wellness," but promoting illness. Instead of sending messages of good health, we are inundated with fear about contracting cancer, heart disease or diabetes. We see commercials regarding about drug interventions and other treatments. By focusing on these constructs, this subconsciously promotes ill health.

One phrase that keeps us stuck in the victim paradigm is "I have to... (fill in the blank)." For example, many say, "I have to work at this job because I have bills to pay," or "I have to stay in this situation because there is nothing else I can do." Remember, everything is a choice. There is truly nothing you ever have to do. We always have hundreds of other options but don't always see them. Oftentimes, we use this phrase because it's a subconscious program that is keeping us stuck in these situations. In addition to the phrase, "I have to...," I have noticed is the overuse of the word "stressed." It appears as though we label everything as stressful: work, life, relationships, the holidays. This is a victim-based concept. Life can be challenging, but things do not have to be stressful. They are only stressful when we label them so. Be mindful of overusing this word. If you find yourself in a challenging situation, before labeling it as stressful, breathe and reframe. You can tell yourself that you will get through this situation and everything will be ok. Remember, you are powerful!

You have the power to find peace even in the midst of adversity by practicing radical acceptance.

A way in which we can shift from feeling like a victim to being empowered is by practicing radical acceptance. One reason that most of us are not feeling peace is that we are judging and not fully accepting our current circumstances. We tend to label our current situation as either good or bad. Situations are neither good nor bad, it is how we label them that makes it so. Buddhist philosophy emphasizes that our suffering is created by our desires and expectations, but once we accept the present moment exactly as it is, our suffering ends, because we have no expectations of how it should be.

There is a prevalent idea in our western world that life should be a certain way. Most of us believe that life should be easy and that we should be happy all the time. However, life will sometimes be difficult, and once we can accept this idea, we can transcend our suffering. M. Scott Peck so eloquently stated in his book The Road Less Traveled, another resource I highly recommend, "Life is difficult, that is a great truth, one of the greatest. It is a great truth because once we truly see this truth, we transcend it. Once we truly know that life is difficult, once we truly understand and accept it, then life is no longer difficult. Because once it is accepted, the fact that life is difficult no longer matters."

Being human means experiencing pain and encountering adversity. Part of finding inner peace is accepting our current reality and minimizing the suffering, which is achieved by accepting it. There is a Buddhist saying, "Pain is inevitable, but suffering is optional." No matter how enlightened we are, we will all experience situations that create feelings of sadness, fear, anger, and frustration, but personal growth is about minimizing not the situation but the suffering. We suffer because instead of accepting our situation and understanding it, we appraise it, consciously and subconsciously, based on our story. Whether we consciously realize it or not, when something triggers an emotion such as sadness, for example after a breakup, we replay our story. Whether we are conscious of it or not, we begin to think, I'm not loveable, I can't do anything right, I'm all alone, which elicits and compounds the negative emotions. This is where we get into the loop of suffering. Inner peace can be found when we start practicing radical acceptance, which means understanding, not attaching to this story, letting go of suffering and accepting instead of judging our current circumstance.

Most of us have expectations of how things "should be," which can cause us distress. We have a picture of how our life should be, how our family should be, how others should treat us, how much money we should be making, what job we should have, etc. These expectations are what create our suffering because, frequently, our present does not resemble what we think it should. We become victims of the images we create and the thoughts that we have about how things should be, which creates un-peacefulness. We often judge how our present should be, but we miss out on appreciating the moment. If you accepted your situation the way it is without judgment, you could eliminate your suffering. This does not mean that you should not try to change your situation, but it means that you can find peace within your present circumstances and make changes without emotional attachment, because judging your reality is truly not productive. When you realize you are not a victim in your life, you can learn to accept your current reality.

Many people worry or get upset about their situation, which in reality is not facilitating anything positive. There is a difference between being concerned about our situation and worrying or being upset about it. Before we can make changes to a situation, it is important to accept it first. Because energetically, if we are not accepting it, we are adding to the negativity associated with the situation. This makes it difficult to attract something different. We don't have to necessarily like it, just accept it. Remember, you created these desires and expectations, so you can eliminate them. You are in control. Inner peace is achieved when we lose our attachment to our desires and can see the reality in our current situation without judgment. You can find peace and appreciate what is instead of lamenting what is not. Letting go of expectations and desires can be quite profound, leading you to feel at peace with your present and help you feel empowered.

You are able to satisfy your emotional needs.

Understanding that you are able to satisfy your own emotional needs is another way in which you are powerful. It is our victim paradigm that we mistakenly believe that the external world is there to satisfy our internal emotional needs, which creates unhealthy dynamics. As mentioned previously, because of subconscious beliefs from childhood, such as feelings of inadequacy, we look to external factors to satisfy these needs. For example, we have expectations that external factors such as other people or a job should make us feel happy, safe or adequate. These are illusions. Happiness, safety and feeling good enough have to come from within. Growing up, psychologically, is letting go of the illusion that the external world is there to take care of you or make you feel better and understanding the only you can resolve internal conflicts. It is also about accepting that you are responsible for your own happiness, contentment, and the outcome of your life.

If we have not resolved internal emotional needs from our childhoods, this also plays out in the relationships we have with others. For example, our childhood dynamic may have contributed to feelings of vulnerability, inadequacy, and anger and instead of resolving it, we seek out ways to overcompensate and sometimes externalize these feelings. Unresolved feelings of inadequacy and anger can manifest in physical abuse, prejudices, hate crimes and the need to control others. I believe this is a huge problem in our society and many of the atrocities in the world are because we have not resolved these childhood conflicts.

There is a concept that I label as the "bully/victim" paradigm, which is an example of this dysfunctional dynamic. Based on our limited experiences, we sometimes believe that there are only two positions in the world, either the bully or victim, which are paradigms learned in childhood. Some children, take on the bully position and externalize their hurt and anger on others, as a way to release this emotion and to feel more empowered. If this child does not resolve this inner conflict, this dynamic followsthem into adulthood. Some ways this is displayed is when othersfeel that controlling or exploiting others is a way to make them feel more powerful and in control. However, the bully is just as disempowered as the victim. The bully will then attract someone who has learned to take the victim position.

There are so many examples, in which this victim/bully paradigm manifests in our lives. For example, a business owner, who hasn't resolved their childhood trauma, will likely control, manipulate and exploit their employees. An employee, who hasn't resolved their childhood trauma, will allow this dynamic and feels stuck in this situation. Or an elected official, who uses their position for personal financial gains without really caring about their constituents, will seek out and find others to manipulate. Narcissism is an example of this bulling paradigm. Individuals with narcissistic tendencies will gravitate toward positions of power. We allow this dynamic to continue to perpetuate because we are conditioned in childhood to engage in this dynamic. We then, seek this out because it is on some level familiar. Additionally, we tend to minimize and distort reality. Because we project our childlike desire for "mommy and daddy," to watchover us, we tend to blindly trust figures of authority as we didour parents because it is too anxiety provoking to be aware that they weren't necessarily protecting us. As a society, we continue perpetuating limiting victim-based beliefs such as "That's just the way it is," or "There is nothing I or anyone else can do about it." However, we can change this by understanding how and why we are stuck in these dysfunctional patterns, believing that there is another way and not engaging in this dynamic.

A wise position is when we realize that there is a third option; to not engage in either role and learn how to satisfy our own emotional needs. A wise person learns how to navigate relationships without being a bully, which means not desiring power or control over others, imposing one's values on others or manipulating others to satisfy internal needs. A wise person also learns how to set boundaries with others and communicate assertively. Because most of us engage in the bully/victim paradigm, assertive communication is something that I have found to most of us don't learn. We learn either aggressive, passive, or passive aggressive communication strategies. Keeping in mind that wise communication is expressed with loving kindness, let's explore the different communication styles through the following example. Your boss asks that you work overtime even though you have been putting in a lot of extra time, feel burnt out and need a break. An aggressive response would be "What the heck! Are you insane? I have been working too much as it is!" An example of a passive response wouldbe, "Sure. I will come in," even though you really don't want to.A passive aggressive example would be, "Sure. I will come in," but then call in sick or purposely mess up at work in retaliation. An assertive response would be "I understand that you want meto work overtime, but I am really burnt out from all the additional work. I really cannot because I need a break."

A wise person also understands that all interactions need to be an equal energetic exchange or a win/win situation because we are all energetically connected. If one party wins and the other party loses, this actually impacts both parties in a negativeway. A bully/victim paradigm appears to be a win/lose but is more accurately a lose/lose position. For example, corporate America often times operates in this win/lose paradigm. To make profits, oftentimes, workers are exploited, the environment is destroyed, and consumers are harmed. This is not a wise business model. It is so important to understand that the negative outcomes created impact everyone. Although some may profit financially from this paradigm, there is a cost to everyone. It is unfortunate that most people do not believe that a business can be both profitable and wise, but this is not so. This is a mistaken belief system that truly needs to be changed. A wise person understands that cooperation is the only solution, and every outcome needs to be a win/win.

Exploring and letting go of addictions is another way we can start feeling empowered. An addiction is defined as a repeated dysfunctional pattern of utilizing an external factor to satisfy an emotional need. We all engage in some type of addiction. Some people escape through drugs and alcohol, thinking that a substance will alleviate feelings of sadness or anxiety. Others escape through social media, TV, technology, sex, religion, shopping, workaholism, relationships, gossip, and other forms of distractions as a way of avoiding pain and emotional discomfort. All of these addictions keep us stuck in patterns of victimization because they reinforce the belief that the only way to cope is through external factors. Our addictions prevent us from dealing with our emotions. It is important to observe and release our addictions as a way of becoming more empowered.

Your self-worth is not defined by external sources.

Our pursuit of validation from outside sources creates suffering and keeps us from feeling empowered. We frequently look to others to validate us or define who we are, or we look for external things such as status, money, or power to define who we are. As with our expectation that external things can provide us with safety or happiness, wanting validation from external sources gives power to external factors, ones usually beyond our control. An important principle to keep in mind is that only you can validate your existence. If you are defining yourself by something external, you will be the victim of this external source. You are giving away your power.

Christina Samycia, PsyD

Here is an exercise: List all the things that you believe validate your existence: your title, your degrees, your friends, your significant other, your family, your paycheck, etc. If you were to throw that list away and no longer had that degree, job, or loved one, would that change who you are? It should not. And if it feels as if it would, this puts you in a powerless place. It is important to understand that these external things can change. Are you giving up your power to external factors? This may be why you may be stuck in certain undesirable situations. For example, you may want to give up that high-paying job to pursue your life passion but are afraid because you believe the title or the paycheck is defining your value. An inherent problem in relationships is that most of us seek validation from our partners. We sometimes want someone else to validate that we are special, possibly because we did not feel as though we received this validation from our parents. We believe that we are special only when someone loves us. However, this gives a lot of power to others. You do not need someone or something else to make you feel special because you already are. Seeking validation from within is another way in which you are powerful.

You are responsible for your health.

Another important paradigm shift is to understand that we are responsible for the condition of our health. I think one of the reasons that we don't take responsibility over our health is due to our philosophy of health. In our western culture, we often feel as though we are victims of "diseases." We are led to believe that illnesses are a result of external factors such as bacteria or viruses or due to genetic factors. The flaw in this theory is that we are bombarded by millions of germs, bacteria, and viruses daily, but become sick only when our immune system is compromised. It becomes compromised due to factors such as emotional and physical stress, nutritional imbalances, or toxic exposure. Additionally, genes may predispose us to certain ailments, but this does not mean we are victims to our genetics. Science has shown that our genes are not fixed but are mutable. Various factors, such as toxins, malnutrition and possibly even our thoughts and feelings can trigger our genes. We also mistakenly believe we are victims to illnesses such as cancer, heart disease and diabetes, because we don't understand how our lifestyle contributes to these illnesses and have been led to believe that they can only be "cured" through pharmaceutical or surgical interventions. However, diseases don't happen to us but develop internally due to imbalances in our system. Illness such as heart disease, diabetes and cancer are largely caused by lifestyle and environmental factors. In fact, 75 percent of our illnesses are lifestyle related, which puts the responsibility on us. Even in regard to psychological conditions, such as depression and anxiety, although there are biochemical and genetic factors that might be contributing to our emotional state, our thoughts, life circumstances, environment and nutritional factors play a large role which is in our hands.

One of the main differences between western and eastern philosophy of health is that the eastern approach is built on the premise that the illnesses occur due to an imbalance in the body and the body has the ability to heal itself. This form of healthcare puts the responsibility on the patient, which is more empowering. An alternative practitioner seeks to find the cause of the problem, not just eliminate or manage the symptoms and implements natural modalities such as herbs, nutritional supplements, dietary modifications, body work and acupuncture which supports the body to heal itself. Because the body has the ability to heal itself, it is so important to understand that all healing is self-healing. No drug, procedure, vitamin, herb, or treatment heals. It only assists the body in doing what it does naturally, which is healing itself. Additionally, eastern alternatives are less invasive and destructive to our bodies than a traditional western approach.

Christina Samycia, PsyD

One of the reasons we don't always take responsibility over our health is that from a psychological perspective, we have this tendency to want someone else, such as "mommy and daddy," to fix things for us. When we were children, we looked to our parents and other adults to help us. When we grow up, we sometimes forget to update this paradigm, and transfer responsibility to others, such as doctors and other health care providers. We look to others to fix our ailments and pain. Some people even identify with their illness and are addicted to the dynamic of seeking others to take care of them. There are also some individuals who would actually die then change their lifestyle. Many are addicted to the substances they use, the food they eat and other lifestyle choices. I have even heard some people say, "Well, if I get a heart attack or cancer, that's ok, the doctors will fix me." Doctors can possibly help, but they are not magicians. When we grow up psychologically, we can begin to understand that we are responsible for our lives, which includes the process of taking care of our health and being in charge of our healing. Health practitioners are there to provide us with tools and wisdom, but we need to do the work. We have the capacity to maintain good health and overcome physical or psychological ailments. This doesn't mean that we will never get sick or die of an illness because sadly our food supply is compromised, our environment is toxic and we will be exposed to pathogens, but we do have a lot of control over other factors. Additionally, some of us, no matter how much we take care of ourselves, will in fact die of illnesses because that may be our life lesson for this lifetime. Although some of this may be inevitable, this doesn't mean we should not do the best we can to take care of ourselves.

The first step to better health is taking responsibility over our health. The second step is believing that it is possible to be healthy and in control of our heath. One of the ways we take responsibility over our health is to start living a healthier lifestyle. We can do this by eating better, resting, managing stress, changing our thinking, exercising and being more mindful of the toxins we expose ourselves to, as well as educating ourselves about our bodies and health. Additionally, part of taking responsibility over your health is looking at the belief systems you have regarding your health. Do you believe that you have the ability to be healthy? Do you want to be healthy? Is there an attachment to being unhealthy, or in pain? Do you believe that getting sick is just a part of life? Do you believe that getting older means being unhealthy? Science has shown us how powerful the mind is over our health. There is much research proving the placebo effect. If we believe it is possible, it usually is. Part of this is not necessarily our fault because we receive so many messages from the medical community that keep us in the victim mentality. These conscious and subconscious beliefs about our health are so important and determine our health status.

Louise Hay is a great resource for understanding the mind-body connection. Her philosophy states that the body is a reflection of subconscious beliefs and it mirrors to us what is out of balance. The body sometimes reflects the belief systems that we hold which is expressed in our illnesses and conditions. For example, if you are struggling with weight, this may be a subconscious need for protection. Throat and thyroid issues can occur if we are not speaking our truth. Back issues and pain can be an indication of lack of support. In her books, she offers ideas about the psychological and spiritual connections to our health and suggests affirmations to help heal the body. According to Traditional Chinese Medicine (TCM), our bodies hold onto emotional responses and stores different emotions in different parts of our bodies known as meridians. For example, fear is located in the kidney meridian, anger in located in the liver meridian, low self-esteem is in the stomach meridian and resentment is in the gallbladder. It may be that unresolved feelings of inadequacy, for example, can lead to stomach disorders or unprocessed fear can impair kidney function.

Reflection

You are powerful. Although you may not always have control over the circumstances in your life, you always have the power to change how you think and feel about them and how you respond to them. Although you don't always have control over all the circumstances in your life, you do contribute to some, if not most of the circumstances that you attract into your life. You are not the victim of yourreality, but the creator of it to some extent. You have the power to find peace, even in the midst of adversity, by practicing radical acceptance. Furthermore, you are able to satisfy your own emotional needsand validate your existence. You also have the power to be healthy, physically, and emotionally, and it's important to start taking responsibility over your health.

Chapter 7

You are Loveable and Good Enough

You are loveable and good enough
exactly the way you are.

Another common belief system that causes us emotional distress is that we are unlovable and not good enough, but this is an important paradigm to shift, as well. You are loveable and good enough exactly the way you are, even if you are not perfect. Everyone is imperfect and everyone is loveable and deserves to be loved. I believe we question if we are loveable because of the messages we received throughout our lives. During our childhood, no matter how wonderful our parents are or were, most of us experienced some conditional love in our childhoods. Remember, everyone has a story. When we are born, our parents project their story onto us. For example, maybe your father was very conservative, perhaps due to his own fears, but you wanted to follow your dream of being an artist. This frightened him, and he tried to change you. In this situation, you might internalize a belief that you are not good enough, but it had nothing to do with you. Or if your parents were abusive, you likely came to the wrong conclusion that you must not be loveable if they are so angry and hurt you. Additionally, this idea of not being good enough is passed down generation to generation. It is highly likely your parents didn't feel conditionally loved and neither did their parents and so on. You may not necessarily be consciously aware of these beliefs because many of these beliefs are internalized.

One of the reasons we don't believe we are loveable or good enough is that we take things personally, which begins in childhood. As children, we truly believed the world revolved around us. We believed that everything that did or did not happen was personal. We still bring some of those ideas into our adult life. In the case of the abusive parent, when that parent is mean to a child, it has nothing to do with the child, it is the anger of the parent. The child is merely the projection of that anger. It is never personal.

As we develop, we continue to measure how loveable we are based on how others treat us. We experience rejection, abandonment, and cruelty and we continue to take it personally. However, nothing is ever personal. Another great resource I highly recommend is The Four Agreements by Don Miguel Ruiz. The second "agreement" in the book is "Don't Take Anything Personally." In it he states, "Nothing other people do is because of you. It is because of themselves. All people live in their own dream, in their own minds; they are in a completely different world from the one you live in." Remember, people do not perceive reality as it is, but as they are. No one really gets to know us because others are constantly projecting their story onto us. We are all just mirrors for other people. Rarely does anyone ever truly see anybody else because we are too involved in our own story and we project that story onto others. How we are treated by others is because of their story and not because of us. We should never define who we are based on the action or words of others. People act in a kind or cruel manner because of who they are. People are only capable of loving others to the extent that they are capable of loving themselves. Whether someone likes you or not, it's not personal. It has nothing to do with us. "If you are willing to look at another person's behavior toward you as a reflection of the state of their relationship with themselves rather than a statement about your value as a person, then you will, over a period of time cease to react at all." Yogi Bhajan. Nothing is ever personal. No matter how anybody has treated you, you are loveable and good enough, exactly the way you are.

We often take things very personally in relationships, especially romantic relationships and tend to suffer when we are rejected. Unless we have done a lot of personal work, most of us will pick partners that reflect dynamics from our childhoods, which is happening on a subconscious level. Therefore, the decisions that others make have nothing to do with us, but about whether we still fit in their story. In most cases, people rarely pick partners that are healthy for them. We usually choose partners to try to resolve some subconscious need that was not met in childhood. Because of this, what most of us think of as love is really about engaging with others in order to satisfy our emotional needs. Now that you are embarking on the process of self-discovery and realizing that you are responsible for satisfying your own emotional needs, you may be wondering, what is love then? I believe M. Scott Peck defines love in such a wonderful way. "Love is the will to extend one's self for the purpose of nurturing one's own or another's spiritual growth...We do not have to love. We chose to love." The way I interpret this, especially as it pertains to romantic love, is that we are all on a spiritual path and each of our paths are separate. We can choose to travel together side by side, always understanding and respecting each other's paths.

No one can love you unconditionally except you.

Another very important paradigm shift is to start practicing unconditional self-love. Louise Hay believes "that there is one thing that heals every problem, and that is to love yourself." She states, "Many of us hide from ourselves and we don't even know who we are. We don't know what we feel, we don't know what we want. Life is a voyage of self-discovery. To me to be enlightened is to do within and to know who and what we really are, and to know that we have the ability to change for the better by loving and taking care of ourselves. It is not selfish to love ourselves. It clears us so that we can love ourselves enough to love other people. We can really help the planet when we come from a space of great love and joy on an individual basis…. Love is the binding agent that holds the whole Universe together… love is deep appreciation. When I talk about loving ourselves, I mean having a deep appreciation for who we are. We accept all the different parts of ourselves, our little peculiarities…the things we may not do so well, and all the wonderful qualities too. We accept the whole package with love. Unconditionally…Love is something we can choose."

When I approach the concept of self-love to my clients, most people are very uncomfortable with it, probably because we were never taught how to love ourselves. We mistakenly believethat only when we are perfect can we love ourselves because deep down inside, most of us never think we are good enough. Something I routinely explain to my clients that can assist in this process is "You don't have to always like parts of yourself or your behavior, but you always have to love yourself. It is about loving the essence of who you are." For example, let's say you engage in unhealthy behaviors such as procrastinating, getting angry, or abusing substances: these behaviors are not you. They are ways you behave. Despite the way you act, which can change, you can always love who you are.

Because we were taught conditional love, part of healing is the process of re-parenting ourselves or becoming a "good mom and dad" to ourselves. Through our psychological development, we internalize imperfect parents. We oftentimes recreate the emotional climate of our childhoods as we tend to treat ourselves like our parents treated us or sometimes the exact opposite, which isn't always better. Part of our healing journey is to make corrections to how we were parented. A good parent does not put a child in harmful situations. For example, are you working at a job that you hate or engaging with abusive people? This is not practicing self-love. We all have a hurt, scared, angry, frustrated little child inside us. Through the process of personal growth, it is important to nurture and heal that child. You can do this by being patient, gentle, understanding and observing, not judging or punishing yourself. Part of loving yourself is also about practicing self-care, such as eating well, exercising, and getting enough sleep. Self-care is also about setting boundaries with others and doing what brings you joy.

Self-love is also about practicing self-acceptance. Louise Hays further states that "Loving yourself begins with never ever criticizing ourselves for anything. Criticism locks us into the very patterns we are trying to change. Understanding and beinggentle with ourselves helps us to move out of it." As I alwayssay to my clients, "Observe, not judge yourself," even if you are engaging in behaviors that you wish to change. Remember, these behaviors are not you. It is always important to see the inner child who is motivating your behavior. Judging or punishing yourself does not facilitate anything positive. Your job is to seek to understand your behavior. Why you are engaging in this behavior is what is important. Once you understand the why, you can choose something different. Would you stop loving a child, judge them, criticize them or punish them if they were engaging in unhealthy behaviors? This would not be healthy or productive. A good parent seeks to understand why the child is engaging in these behaviors and helps them find a better solution. Again, seek to become a good parent to yourself. Every child deserves to be loved, even you, especially you.

Self-love is also about being kinder to yourself which starts with paying attention to the things you say to yourself. As mentioned earlier, everything is energy. Your thoughts are energy. If you have negative thoughts about yourself, this disrupts your energetic and biochemical system, which is detrimental to your health. This is why it is so important to pay attention to those things you say to yourself and practice changing them. When you begin listening to the things you say to yourself, you will likely begin to notice how mean you are to yourself. Would you ever say those things to anyone else? Probably not. Remember your inner child and be kind to him or her.

I think one reason why many of us have a difficult time with self-love is that many people confuse self-love with narcissism. Narcissism is not the same as loving yourself. Narcissism is about only thinking of yourself and needing to feel better than others, which actually stems from a deep-seated belief of not being good enough. Loving yourself is not being self-centered or narcissistic, because only when you truly love yourself can you really love and care about others. When you love yourself, you don't compare yourself to anyone else. When you love yourself, you don't seek power over others or to be better than anyone else. When you truly love yourself, you also want what is best for others. I also believe that some people are afraid to love themselves as a means of self-control. Some confuse self-love with self-indulgence, but when you truly love yourself, you do not harm yourself by overindulging, like good parent who doesn't indulge a child with cake for dinner. You practice moderation. You provide a balanced meal with a little treat. That is love. Love is never indulgent.

If you are not still comfortable with loving yourself because it feels "selfish," here is another way to look at it. Loving yourself is actually helping the world around you. As we have discovered, we are all energy, and energy affects surrounding energy. Therefore, we are all connected in an energetic way. Healing our emotional scars, loving ourselves, and being happy and at peace is actually part of our spiritual commitment to the universe, because we are adding something positive to the universe. We are all connected. All too often, we feel that self-love, being happy or at peace is "selfish," but if we are part of a greater whole, we need to love ourselves just as much as we love others. Because we impact the world around us, being unhappy or living with fear, guilt or anger is in a sense adding negativity to our world. Therefore, it is altruistic to be happy and at peace, which we accomplish first by healing our wounds and learning how to really love ourselves. This world can definitely benefit from more love!

Practice unconditional love for others.

Just like it is so important to practice self-love, it is also important to practice unconditional love for others. We can achieve this by seeking to understand others and be patient with them. Just as our unresolved emotional scars dictate our behavior, others experience the same dynamic. It is not uncommon that, once you understand your dynamic, you want others to be the same way. However, it is important to understand that others are not necessarily on the same path as you. It is impossible to change someone who is not seeking change. It is important not to have expectations and think that we can change others. All we can do is serve as an example and share with others who are interested in sharing. Remember that your expectations and the negative emotions they elicit are only hurting you. Judging others, such as thinking someone is a "bad" person, creates negative energy that only hurts you. Righteous anger is still anger and it negatively impacts you and the world around you. Keep in mind that there are no "bad" people because at our core we are all spiritual beings. Therefore, we are all connected and perfect, but acting imperfectly in the human form due to our ego. People are just behaving badly, or at least in our perception, due to their emotional circumstances, such as hurt, anger and fear. We behave in certain ways based on our story. When you

73

come from a place of understanding, not judging, this is a place of peace. One way to let go of negative emotions towards other people is to look for that inner child that is scared, hurt, angry or sad within them. It is helpful to imagine others as little children who are just replaying the human drama. Hopefully, this can shift you from anger, hurt, and frustration, to compassion, love and understanding.

Reflection

You are loveable and good enough. Because nothing is ever personal, we cannot measure how lovable or good enough we are based on external sources. No matter what anyone has ever told you or how they have treated you, you are good enough and de- serve to be loved. The only person who is going to love you unconditionally is you and this needs to be practiced. We also need to practice unconditional love for others. Remember that they are going through the same struggles you are.

Chapter 8

You Are Safe

Fear is an illusion.

Another major paradigm shift is to remember that you are always safe. Fears are not real. They only exist in the mind. Fear is about some future incident that may or may not happen. It'san illusion. If you are experiencing anxiety or have an anxiety provoking thought, it is helpful to remember that although anxiety feels real, it's not because nothing is really happeningto you. You are always safe in the present moment. A lot of our subconscious and conscious fears keep us trapped in situations that are creating unhappiness. For example, if you are staying at a job that you hate because you fear that you won't get hired anywhere else, this is not real. Or if you are staying in an abusive relationship because you fear being alone, this too is not reality. These are illusions. I think it is so important to do what you love and be in healthy situations, not what makes you feel safe. This is the difference between merely surviving and thriving.

Worry harms the body. I believe people worry because it creates a false sense of doing something. People who worry inaccurately believe that if I am worrying about something, I am taking action. However, worrying facilitates absolutely nothing positive and actually impairs your problem-solving capabilities. If you find yourself worrying, breathe, get centered and remind yourself that everything is ok, and you are safe in the present moment. In the next section, I will be providing you with techniques to help you process anxiety

One fear that creates anxiety for many of us is the irrational belief of scarcity. Because of our experiences and the messages, we receive from others, we create inaccurate beliefs that there is not enough money, love, opportunities, etc. in the world and we worry about not having enough. However, the universe is abundant and again, according to the law of attraction, we manifest that which we pay attention to. If you believe that there is not enough money, money will be an issue. If you believe that there is not enough love, love will be an issue. Therefore, instead of worrying about these concepts, which facilitates nothing positive and harms the body, start practicing changing these inaccurate beliefs.

Worrying and feeling anxious is not necessarily the same thing. It is important to discern if the anxiety you are feeling is followed by a thought or if the anxiety you are experiencing is stemming from another source. If your anxiety seems to come out of nowhere, it could be either that a subconscious construct triggered an emotional response or that this feeling of anxiety is a signal that you are not in a situation that is safe or desirable for you. If you are an empath, this can also mean that you may be feeling someone else's anxiety. It is important to get clarity on the source of anxiety because it just may be that this is your subconscious mind trying to alert you to something that you are not paying attention to. Here are some examples to illustrate the difference.

If you start to feel sick and begin ruminating about the possibility of having a horrible illness and this creates anxiety, this is an example of worrying. You can change the thought, which can change the emotional response. However, sometimes changing the thought does not change the emotional response, which indicates that it is likely triggering unprocessed emotional trauma which can be processed. This will be discussed in the next section. However, if you interact with a person and you tend to feel anxiety about it for no apparent reason, this may be your subconscious alerting you that interacting with this person is not healthy for you or that you may be picking up their anxiety. Depending on the nature of the anxiety, this will determine your course of action, which will be expanded on in a future section. However, the emotional clearing exercises listed will be useful in most cases.

Start practicing life-affirming, not fear-based living.

To begin practice life-affirming living, it is important to fully embrace the idea that death is part of life. In our western world, the greatest fear that is not widely discussed is the fear of death. However, it is important to confront this fear because it's the basis of most fears. Death is usually perceived to be negative. Most people don't want to face it and go to great lengths to avoid it, which of course, is not possible. It may be that we are just too attached to the material world, which makes it difficult for us to understand that everything is temporary, even our material body. It is so important to truly embrace the reality that you and everyone else at some point will die. We usually don't know when and how, but it is the inevitable truth of being human. Because of our fear of death, many of us people spend time and energy worrying about being safe and the safety of others to ensure that nothing will happen to themselves or to the one's they love. Of course, you should take precautions such as look both ways before you cross a street or wear your seat belt while driving but living with the constant fear of death is just not a healthy way to live. Because we are spiritual beings, there truly is no death since the essence of who you are is immortal. There is only death to the material manifestation of who we are. Therefore, there is truly nothing to fear, and you are always safe.

According to existential psychology, to move forward in one's personal growth, it is essential to embrace the idea that we are all going to die. Death is the only thing in life that we are certain of, and we don't know exactly when it will happen, nor can we prevent it despite all of our best efforts. One of the reasons that we fear death is that we fear the unknown and the idea of not being. Death is in the future and our preoccupation with it keeps us from living. However, the idea that we die can spark us to appreciate every moment we have, primarily by causing us to make choices not based on fear but based on thriving and living in a life-affirming way.

Most of us do not want to think about death, but by confronting death, we can begin to live a full, authentic, happy life. To live life fully, it is important to accept that it ends. It is sometimesin the face of death that we begin to truly live. A confrontation with death often causes us to question what is meaningful and important. As existentialist psychotherapist Irvin Yalom said, "Although the physicality of death destroys man, the idea of death saves him." Have you ever heard someone that has been diagnosed with a life-threatening illness say, "I wish I had spent more time working"? Almost everybody says, "I wish I'd spent time doing the things I wanted to do; traveling, spending time with others, being closer with my family, having fun." Many individuals experience life-altering changes after being confronted with their mortality, such as having someone close to them die or having been diagnosed with a terminal illness. These circumstances remind us that life is temporary and we should start living it.

When you start to think about the choices you make, you will find that you make many decisions out of fear, which keeps you from living fully. Most of us live in fear and we make decisions based on fear rather than making life affirming choices. Think about the decisions that you make: are they truly positive and life-affirming, or are they created out of fear; fear of being hurt,

Christina Samycia, PsyD

fear of failure or success, fear of the unknown? Most of these fears are rooted in inaccurate belief systems from our past and from those around us. Living in a life-affirming way is the difference between thriving and merely surviving. Our fears keep us from living authentically. Instead of working at a job that you hate or being in an unfulfilling relationship because you believe that you need security, while wondering if you can do something you love or find more meaningful connections, choose activities and connections that bring you contentment, joy, and something that you look forward to when you wake up in the morning. Part of self-love is never staying in situations that make you unhappy. There is no such thing as security or safety in external things. These are illusions because everything in the end is temporary. What do you do out of fear? What changes can you make to live in a more life-affirming way?

You are connected and therefore never alone.

Another reason we don't feel safe is that we feel the anxiety and sadness of loneliness. However, loneliness is a psychological construct. It is not reality. It just feels real. Remember, we are energy. Our spiritual energetic self is always connected to everything. Therefore, we are never truly alone, we just sometimes feel alone. It is our ego self that feels separate from others and yearns for connectedness. It is important to understand this feeling of loneliness and transcend it by realizing that we are only alone in the sense that we view our experience of the world as separate. However, we are always connected to a greater whole. You can overcome this aloneness and conquer the fear of being alone by understanding that this is only an ego construct, not reality.

In my years of working with clients, I have discovered that one of the most common experiences is the feeling of loneliness and not fitting in. I don't think that I have ever encountered one person who ever felt like they truly belonged. I feel that loneliness is a spiritual yearning for connectedness which comes from our childhood need for dependency and fear of abandonment. As children, belonging to a family was paramount to our survival. Being unloved or unwanted is a life-or-death situation. We could not survive alone in the world. However, as we grow up, we forget to move beyond this fear. We all want to be connected to a group, but we all already belong because we are all already connected. Therefore, you are never alone.

Reflection

You are always safe. Fear is about somefuture incident that may or may nothappen. It's an illusion. It is important tostart practicing life-affirming living. Oneway to do this is to embrace the fact thateverything material is temporary. Becauseyou are a spiritual being in a material body, you are always safe because the essence of who you are is eternal. Loneliness is also merely a psychological construct because you are always connected.

Chapter 9

You Are Wise

Learn to trust your inner wisdom.

Another major paradigm shift is to understand that you are wise. Most of us tend to seek answers outside of ourselves, because we have been taught that is where to find it. It is unlikely that anyone has ever taught you how wise you truly are and how to tap into that inner wisdom. It is also highly unlikely that anyone has ever shown you a different way of living, by looking inward for the answers. Although it is wise to seek guidance, ultimately, you need to do what's best for you and only you know what that is.

"Life is complex. Each one of us must make his (or her) own path through life. There are no self-help manuals, no formulas, no easy answers…The journey of life is not paved in blacktop. It is not brightly lit, and it has no road signs. It is a rocky path through the wilderness," M. Scott Peck. I think one of the reasons we search for wisdom outside of ourselves is because we are afraid to take responsibility and possibly make mistakes. Because of our fears, we tend to manage our lives based on what others think is best. However, we all have inner wisdom and a unique path, and no one can really show us how to live our lives. There is a Buddhist proverb that states, "Believe nothing, no matter where you read it, or who said it, no matter if I have said it, unless it agrees with your own reason and your own common sense." It is always valuable to check in with our inner wisdom and to always trust ourselves.

One of the ways to access inner wisdom is through our intuition, which is one of our most valuable assets. It's the voice of our subconscious mind also known as the higher self, which is connected to a collective unconscious. Therefore, we all have access to universal information. However, most of us do not know that it even exists. That is why it is so important to learn how to access it. One way is to learn how to sit still and access our intuition. You can learn how to ask the questions and look for what intuitively feels right, which can be learned through techniques such as meditation.

There is a power technique that I teach my clients, which is not only helpful in making decisions, but extremely helpful in accessing subconscious material. It is so simple, yet so profoundly effective. All you need to do is get into a relaxed state, close your eyes and take a few deep breaths. Then ask the question and wait to see how your body responds. For example, if you are wondering if a job is the right one for you, with your eyes closed, say either out loud or to yourself, "This is the right job for me." Then wait to see how you feel. Usually, the response is immediate. Sometimes you can't even say it out loud because there is so much resistance. If it is the right job for you, when you say it, there will be no resistance. It will feel right. Again, you have all the answers, you just need to sit still, uncover them and trust. Something that I have learned throughout the years is to also be patient when making a decision. We often make a choice when we don't have a clear yes. However, I believe that if it is not a clear yes, it's a no. It is wise to be patient and wait for the option that resonates with a clear yes.

You can also use this technique to test belief systems, which will be helpful in the next section where we will be working on clearing limiting beliefs. For example, if you are struggling with relationships, you may find it helpful to test your beliefs regarding relationships. Your beliefs may be the obstacle in attracting as well as holding onto relationships. When testing subconscious belief systems, the first thing I have my clients do is close their eyes and say, "I am okay being in a relationship." You will be surprised how often a client will swear that they truly want one, but when they do this exercise, there is so much resistance. Using this "okay" statement is so useful because if you are not okay with love, money, or whatever you think you are seeking, it will be difficult to obtain. These beliefs will impact your decisions and what you attract. You can then proceed further as to why relationships, money or whatever are not ok. Sometimes, we are not okay with relationships because we are afraid to lose them. Sometimes, we are not okay with money because we are afraid that we will seem greedy. I then help my clients systematically clear these belief systems by detaching energetically from them, which will be covered in the next section.

Intuition is where logic and emotion meet. It's the wise mind. All too often, we make decisions based on just logic. We spend hours thinking and researching but logic and information such as statistics relies on others' past truths that may not necessarily apply to you. For example, if you are thinking of getting a new job you need to find that middle ground between the logical and emotional. If you find a job that pays well and has great benefits, but you hate it, that is not the right job. If you find a job that you enjoy, but you can barely pay the bills, that one is not right either. The best job is the one that satisfies both criteria. This is also true with relationships. We tend to pick a partner for logical reasons, such as they "look good on paper;" you've checked all the right boxes but maybe you don't feel an emotional connection. Or we pick someone that we feel emotionally connected with, but they are irresponsible or emotionally unstable, and not logically a good choice. The wise choice is one that meets both the logical and emotional needs.

It is important to discover your authentic self.

Part of embracing our inner wisdom is to uncover our authentic self. According to existential psychology, the existential aim in life is the individual's search for meaning and purpose through the discovery of one's authentic self. This purpose is part of our spiritual path and often we are conflicted between our soul's path and what others want us to be. Being authentic is living as who we are, not by the roles that we have designed for ourselvesor that others have created for us. We are all born authentic but spend a significant amount of time wearing masks. We learnto wear these masks because we want to please those around us and to feel safe. When we go out into the world, instead of being ourselves, we desire approval, acceptance, and love fromothers and feel we need to wear masks to get that approval. Weplay a role because we are afraid or ashamed to be our true selves. These roles are taken from images we develop of how we should be, and are dictated by others such as our parents, friends, peers, or the media. Being authentic is taking off the masks that you wear and being the person who you truly are.

On some level, we all know why we are here and what we are supposed to learn and experience, but out of fear, we sometimes resist it. We try to be what others want us to be. Sometimes we are afraid to disappoint others or make others feel bad or uncomfortable. However, sometimes emotional distress suchas unhappiness and anxiety is a signal that we are not on our authentic path. It is our higher-self or subconscious-self giving us a signal that we might not be headed in the right direction.

The key to living authentically is filtering out those other voices in your mind and finding your authentic voice. At any given moment, it seems there are several voices in your head: your authentic voice, the voice of your family, a societal voice and conflicted subconscious information. All these voices, bouncing off one another, can create inner conflict, so it is important to find your authentic voice and cast off the others. Is there something you truly would like to do, but are conflicted or fearful about? For example, are you unhappy with your current career choice, and have you always dreamt of something else, but wondered about its feasibility or practicality or believed that you may disappoint your family? It is important to determine whose voices are spreading this doubt. If your authentic self truly wants to pursue something different, it may be helpful to challenge the voices of your family and society, which may have created your fear. There will always be an inner conflict as long as we act to please others or do what is expected, instead of following our authentic voice. Therefore, one of the steps to inner peace is filtering out those other voices in our head and allowing the authentic self to emerge.

Once you choose to follow your authentic voice, you may feel some tension. This is perfectly normal, because frequentlyit is fear that has dictated your behavior. It takes courage to be authentic, and your choices truly determine the person you want to become. You have the freedom to create your own life. To be authentic also means to create your own definition of success, not what society or others deem as successful. You are responsible for your actions, but also for your failure to act. This discovery can be anxiety-provoking because it awakens the realization that you have the responsibility to take control over your life and your destiny. But once you start practicing authenticity, this anxiety will diminish.

Part of being authentic is finding personal meaning in our lives. By living with our beliefs, we know the direction that we are meant to go, and we trust the universe will lead the way. As we learned earlier, only we can validate our existence and we must not give that power to others. This means we create our own idea of personal success and meaning in our lives. We can free ourselves from cultural expectations and create our own life, full of personal meaning. When we find meaning and purpose, all the anxiety and hopelessness and fear disappear. Our mission guides us. We become aware that we have authorship of our lives and start to take responsibility over our destiny, feelings, and even our suffering. We then create our own life meaning by creating our unique purpose in life.

Understanding who we are authentically.

Because we start to wear masks at an early age, it can be challenging to uncover who we are authentically. I have discovered two very useful tools, astrology and numerology, that can aid in helping us understand our authentic life path. Astrology is something that is very much misunderstood in our western world. Many have associated it with superstition and fortunetelling. However, astrology is a psychological and counseling tool, which can be used for enhancing personal wellbeing. Carl Jung, a prominent psychiatrist and psychoanalyst, who is credited for his theories of personality extensively researched the field of astrology and even consulted the I Ching and read tarot cards.

According to The Astrology Bible by Judy Hall, "The zodiac is not simply the celestial path of the Sun – it is a voyage through the human experience. It represents the journey of the soul (The Sun) from its conception through childhood and old age." The journey begins as our soul comes into incarnation in Aries. This is where the ego and the awareness of self begins. In Taurus, our soul's journey is through experiencing the physical body. When we enter Gemini, our soul learns how to communicate with the world. In Cancer, our soul learns how to nurture others. Moving into Leo, our soul seeks recognition for its creation. Virgo represents our soul's journey of learning how to serve to others and structure a daily routine. In Libra, our soul learns how to relate and compromise with others. In Scorpio, the soul begins to recognize its regenerative nature. In Sagittarius, the soul searches for meaning. Capricorn represents the soul's drive to be responsible for others through hard work. In Aquarius, the soul's quest is for humanitarian efforts. When the soul reaches Pisces, its desire is to merge the spiritual. It is believed that we incarnate several times throughout this cycle.

According to spiritualists, it is believed that we choose the exact time and date of our birth. Our natal chart is our spiritual blueprint, which is the snapshot of the sky the moment we are born. The date of birth shows where the sun, moon and planets are located, and the time of birth indicates the position of this placement. Our natal chart gives us clues as to the life lessons we are to learn, our personality traits, our soul's purpose, and our inherent energies and temperament as well as challenges we might face. Although everyone has free-will, that will determine their destiny, one's natal chart can indicate how someone is liable to think and react to a particular set of circumstances. One's natal chart is useful for understanding one's natural reactions and to aid in making healthier life decisions. It is important to understand that astrology is a language of symbols and should not be taken literally. Because the natal chart has so many aspects, this explains why two individuals with the same sun sign are not necessarily alike. Although our natal chart is very complicated, I will illustrate a few important indicators that can be helpful in understanding who you are authentically and why you are here. These placements include the sun, moon, rising orascending sign and the nodes.

Our sun sign indicates our inner personality, something we don't always allow others to see, also known as the ego. Most of us know our sun sign, which represents our core personality. Aries, for example, is the first sign, whose personality is usually assertive and dynamic. Aries is a cardinal fire sign, which implies an inclination about initiating creation and change. Whereas, Pisces, the last sign, is extremely sensitive, intuitive, and compassionate. Pisces is mutable water, which implies an adaptability to the environment and someone who feels emotions deeply.

The rising sign or ascending sign indicates our particular outlook on life. The rising sign is the sign that is ascending over the horizon at the time of our birth. It is our particular viewpoint based on the circumstances of our birth, the conditions of the environment we are born into and how we choose to survive during our childhood. The rising sign is as important as the sun sign because it's the mask we wear in the world and how we choose to express our core personality. With a Gemini rising, for example, one's main objective is to communicate with the world, choosing intellect and skills in communication as a means of survival. However, someone with a Virgo rising, for example, seeks to serve others, choosing hard work and structure as a means of survival.

The moon represents our unconscious drives as well as our emotional climate. It pertains to basic needs that arise from the subconscious. If one's moon is in Taurus, for example, there is an inclination to be emotionally fixed, maternal, and craving security. Whereas a moon in Sagittarius, the emotional climate is more restless needing to seek freedom and adventure in the world.

Our north node is the life path or what we need to accomplish in this lifetime in order to fulfil one's destiny. The south node are the lessons we learned in previous incarnations that will aid in fulfilling our mission in this lifetime. Someone with a north node in Aquarius, for example, is destined to help humanity in their lifetime. Their south node would then be in Leo which represents mastering the ego and obtaining personal power in previous reincarnations. A north node in Capricorn is the path of self-discipline and hard work in this lifetime having mastered the south node's lessons in Cancer to nurture and protect others.

In addition to these four important placements, there are other planets that influence us. Venus, for example, represents our attitude with love. Someone with a Venus in Libra, for example, desires a significant other and may fall easily in love. Mars reveals how assertive we are. Having a Mars in Scorpio, for example, symbolizes someone with powerful assertiveness. Where our sun, moon, rising sign and other planets sit in our chart, referred to as houses, this is how we express ourselves through both that sign and house it is positioned in. The twelve houses correspond to the 12 zodiac signs. Aries is the first sign and the first house. The first house represents our individuality and soul's expression. The second house, Taurus, represents material wealth and possessions. The third house represents communication. It is advised that you work with an astrologer to aid in interpreting your chart keeping in mind that everyone has their own interpretation. Trust your intuition as to whatinformation resonates with you.

Numerology is another valuable tool that can help us understand our authentic life path. As in astrology, numerology has many facets but one of the most important numbers is our life path number. To calculate your life path number, you reduce each unit of your birth date; month, day, and year, into a single-digit number or a master number (11, 22 or 33). Then add the numbers together until you get a single digit or master number. For example, someone born on January 1, 2019, their life path number would be 5. It would be calculated $1 + 1 + (2+0+1+9 = 12$, then $1+3 = 3$). Here is a brief description what each life path represents.

Life path 1 is the primal force. Individual with this life path are hard workers and born leaders. They are independent and are meant to follow their own path. Individuals born with

Christina Samycia, PsyD

a life path 2 are the peacemakers. They seek truth, peace, and harmony. Having a life path 3 is living a creative life and achieving self-expression through communication and art. They are independent, playful and have an abundance of creative energy. Those with a life path 4 are the builders and worker bees. They are grounded, serious, and hard working. Life path 5 is the dynamic force. They tend to seek freedom and change and are free spirited and adventurous. Life path 6 are the caretakers. They are incredibly nurturing and are responsible and aware of others. Those with a life path 7 are here to seek a higher awareness. They are the seekers of truth, the thinkers and are on a spiritual path. Individuals with life path 8 are here to achieve balance and power. They are excellent business executives and represent material wealth and ambition. Life path 9 is the number of global awareness and completion. They are the humanitarians and take charge and care of others. Those with a life path 11 are very intuitive. They are sensitive, spiritually aware and understanding of others. Individuals with a life path 22 are the visionaries. They have great spiritual understanding and ability to apply this information in a practical way. Lastly, lifepath 33 are the master teachers and the spiritual leaders. They are altruistic and focused on raising the consciousness of others.

Reflection

You are wise. Most of us tend to seek wisdom outside of ourselves, because we have been taught that it is where to find itbut tapping into our intuition is one way to access inner wisdom. Part of our wisdom is being and trusting our authentic selfwhich can be done by filtering all the voices in our minds and leading with theauthentic one. Astrology and numerology are useful tools in helping us discover our authentic life path.

Chapter 10

You Are a Spiritual Being

Many things that have happened in your life are part of your spiritual journey.

Another paradigm shift is to embrace that we are spiritual beings having a human experience. According to many spiritual teachings, it is believed that we are here on this planet to learn life lessons in order to evolve spiritually. If we are here to learn through our experiences, the situations we encounter are part of our spiritual journey. Understanding this can help you find peace and acceptance, especially in the midst of adversity. "You must be willing to meet existential suffering and work through it. In order to do this, the attitude toward pain has to change. This happens when we accept the fact that everything that happens to us has been designed for our spiritual growth." M. Scott Peck.

As mentioned previously, many spiritual teachings subscribe to the concept of reincarnation and karma. We come backlifetime after lifetime to learn lessons to evolve in our spiritual development. We also sometimes return to help others with their path. Planet earth can be seen as a school. All of us learning different lessons at different lifetimes. Each of us in different classes, learning at different rates through our experiences. All of us are essentially learning from each other. Through relationships, adversity, suffering and our life experience, we grow. We all have to experience different aspects of human existence with the goal of learning love, compassion and understanding in the human form. We will all experience being poor, rich, man, woman, different religions, races, and life circumstances. In his book, Messages for the Masters, a book I highly recommend as well as Many Lives, Many Masters, Brian Weiss explains, "When people have intense spiritual experiences, the energy of love is nearly always evoked. This form of love is unconditional, absolute, and transcendent...Love is the most basic and pervasive energy that exists. It is the essence of our being and of our universe. Love is the fundamental building block of nature connecting and unifying all things, all people. Love is more than a goal, more than a fuel, more than an ideal. Love is our nature. We are love.... The messages of the Masters...reminds us to allow our mindsto return to what is important - love, peace, eternal life, spiritual thoughts and practices — and put aside what is unimportant - material things, pride and ego, violence, fear, worry and hatred."

Some spiritualists believe that before we are born, we decide what lessons need to be learned in that lifetime. We pick the family and life circumstances that will best facilitate those lessons. Often time our life circumstances reflects that life lesson that we need to learn. Some of us will do, what some might define as "bad" things such as murder, theft, betrayal to learn the lesson in that lifetime. Some of us will do what we would define as "good", sometimes to rectify the "bad" thingswe did in past lifetimes. The idea of karma is something that we have oversimplified and is oftentimes misunderstood. Most people believe that karma implies that if you do either a good orbad deed in a lifetime, you will either be rewarded or punished inthe next. As I stated before, we are not victims. There is nothingor no one out there rewarding or punishing us. We are the judgeand jury. Karma does not happen to us, we choose it. Karma is something we choose to experience in a lifetime in order to learn whatever we need to learn in that lifetime. Sometimes we choose a particularly challenging lifetime in order to accelerate our spiritual growth. Therefore, a hard life is not a punishment but rather an opportunity for more growth. This is not to mean that if you are experiencing adversity in your life, you consciouslychose or deserve it. More importantly it is about understanding the lessons that need to be learned through this experience. Blaming and judging is not helpful.

Because the circumstances in our lives may be part of our spiritual journey, it is useful to keep in mind that you and your life are exactly how they are supposed to be right now and that many of the experiences you are encountering are part of this journey. Although this may be difficult to accept during a time of adversity, keep in mind that there is a reason that you and the universe have created the situation you are in right now. There is a Buddhist proverb that states "Nothing ever goes away until it teaches us what you have to learn." Through your experiences, you are learning valuable life lessons. And instead of judging them and feeling like a victim, embrace them and realize that at some time you will understand the lesson to be learned. Although it is ok to feel sad, angry, or frustrated at your situation, it is important not to stay there, but to discover what you are supposed to learn about yourself through this experience. And once you do, the circumstance usually changes.

Something I have to continually remind myself is, "My life is perfect, with all of its imperfections. I have exactly everything I need right now. My life is exactly how it needs to be at the present." Inner peace is found when you accept your life as it is in that particular moment, and not in desiring it to be anything different from what it is. Even during the most trying times, you can accept the present for what and how it is without judgment and learn the lesson that is the result of the situation. You can learn to understand that the universe never gives you something you cannot handle. The situation is temporary, and it too shall pass. You can learn to trust that the universe is providing you with all that you need at the moment. Even in the most trying times, it is important to embrace the present exactly how it is and trust that what you are going through in the moment is important for personal and spiritual growth. This can help us move from victimhood to becoming empowered by the situation we are in.

It is believed that after we die our souls leave our bodies and our learning continues on higher planes of consciousness. We review the lives we have just left, learn our lessons, and plan for our next life. "We choose when we will come into our physical state and when we will leave. We know when we have accomplished what we were sent down here to accomplish… When you have had the time to rest and re-energize your soul, you are allowed to choose your re-entry back into the physical state." Brian Weiss.

Accept and forgive the past.

In addition to accepting our present, it is equally important to accept our past, no matter how terrible it was, and understand that those circumstances were also part of our spiritual journey. Many of us curse the past, hate the things that have happened, detest those who have wronged us, and question why these things happened to us, which leads us to feel victimized. No matter how terrible the trauma, it is important to find acceptance, because some of these situations may be part of our spiritual journey. Realistically, the past does not exist. It is only a figment of our minds. Furthermore, there is nothing we can do about our past, and being upset about it does not change things. Judging the past only creates pain for you in the present.

Many times, we hold on to the hurt, anger and resentment of our past because we want to punish those who have wronged us. But being angry only punishes us in the present. We also believe that by holding on to these emotions, this will protect us in the present. But our past has nothing to do with our present or future unless we allow it. We cannot change the past; all we can change is how we feel about it in the present, and not accepting it is only negatively impacting us in the present. We can learn to embrace our past and show gratitude for those experiences, no matter how terrible. Without those experiences, we would not be who we are. It is in the face of adversity that we grow. Very little growth is achieved when things are going well for us. Without trauma, conflict, and obstacles we would have no opportunities for growth. When we understand this, we can look back on our past and be grateful for these experiences of personal growth.

Part of accepting our past is to forgive those that have hurt us. Sometimes, we find it hard to forgive others because we want to punish those who wronged us. However, holding onto this anger only punishes you. There is a Buddhist saying, "Holding on to anger is like grasping a hot coal with the intent of throwing it at someone else; you are the one who gets burned." Forgiving is really a gift that we give ourselves. Forgiveness is not a weak or passive act, but one of courage. By forgiving, you take your power back and begin living in the present moment. To feel at peace, it is important to forgive others. Often, we confuse forgiving with agreeing. However, you can still believe that if someone hurt you, what they did was wrong, and you can forgive. Letting go ofthe anger is not condoning what has happened. We also often confuse forgiveness with forgetting. When you forgive, you don't forget what has happened, but the negative emotions no longer follow the memory. Remember, forgiveness is not an emotion, but a choice. A choice that is important in finding peace. Sometimes we have difficulty forgiving, because we still desire that person to right the wrong, they committed. But, as mentioned earlier, those expectations cause us pain. We cannot right the wrong that has happened. Being angry, bitter, and resentful keeps us stuck in a victim mentality. Furthermore, we need to remember that those experiences are possibly situations that we needed to experience for our personal and spiritual development.

However, when working through painful experiences, itis valuable not to forgive too quickly. Some say, for example, "My parents did the best they could, and I forgive them," before examining the many facets of their childhood experiences. In order to fully process the pain, it is important to fully acknowledge all the ways in which you were wronged before forgiving. Forgiving too quickly prevents us from fully processing all the hurt, sadness and anger. Once you have let go of the pain, the process of forgiveness becomes easier. Sometimes, we can also seek forgiveness once we understand why others did what they did. Others hurt us because they have not dealt with their own emotional demons and sometimes people just do horrible things. Again, remember that nothing is personal.

Shifting from ego-based to spiritual-based living.

Because you are a spiritual being in a material body, it is important to shift from ego-based living to spiritual-based living. Spiritual-based living is the process of exploring who and what we are, and how we are all alike and connected together as humans. It is identifying the essence of who we are and living from our deepest nature, which includes being consciously aware of our thoughts and feelings and the impact we have on the world. Spiritual-based living is living in harmony with the universe and understanding that our spiritual essence is energy, and we are all interconnected.

Once we understand that we are all connected, we can start to perceive others, as well as our place within the universe, in a different light. It is our ego that feels separate from others and the universe, which creates distress. Distress comes in when we feel isolated and separate from the rest of the world and when we believe in an "I" against the world idea. When we shift from ego-based living to spiritual-based living, we can embrace the idea that I am part of the whole. There is safety and trust and hence no distress. There is trust that everything will work out. When we trust, we can learn that when obstacles come our way, there is a spiritual reason for it. Everything that enters your world can now be seen as a lesson to be learned, not something that you need to be upset over.

Once we shift from ego-based to spiritual-based living, we can also become more compassionate with others and understand that we are connected to one another, leading us to love each other, not hate or judge, because we understand that hatred and judgment is negative energy that hurts us just as much as it hurts others. When we hate or are angry, this just generates negativity within our universe. It is sometimes difficult to not judge and be angry when we see injustice and when others are suffering. However, peace can be attained when we understand that some, if not many, things happen for a reason, even the terrible things. We can learn to understand that others are experiencingwhat is necessary for their spiritual development and judgingor hating those who are "bad" is still bringing negativity to our world. We can find compassion and understanding when we understand that others are possibly just following their karma. Although we may not agree with their actions, we can learn tolet go of anger and judgement. "Learning how to love is the goaland the purpose of spiritual life, not learning how to develop psychic powers, not learning how to bow, chant, do yoga, or even meditate, but learning to love. Love is the Truth. Love is theLight." Lama Surya Das.

When we can put aside the ego, we come from a place of wisdom, and are able to see a bigger picture. We are able to see that we are part of a bigger whole and can make decisions that do not merely satisfy the needs of the ego. We can put things in perspective. We can see how insignificant some of the drama that we encounter truly is in the grand scheme of things. Letting go of the ego allows us to enjoy the simple things and be grateful for what we have, not what we do not have. This concept of letting go of our ego is essentially preparing us for the ultimate letting go—death. Once we fully embrace our spiritual side, we no longer fear death, because our spirit, the essence of who we are, will always be there, even though our physical aspect may not. There is a peacefulness to be found when we understand this because much of the anxiety that we have centers on the fear of death. But if we embrace the essence of who we are, death is just the end of the material part of who we are. If we are not attached to the materiality of who we are, we can find peace in knowing that we are in a sense immortal. As we know, energy cannot be destroyed nor created, only transformed. Therefore, the essence of who you are has and always will be. Death is only the death of the physical part of who we are, not the spiritual part.

There is power in the universal flow of things and being spiritual is trusting this. It is not that we are powerless, because as mentioned before, we are the creators, but it is in our best interest to sometimes surrender and go with the flow. It is about working with the universe, not against it. If we are trying too hard, this is out of fear, which prevents us from manifesting what we want. It is not that we should not have goals, but to trust that the universe will provide a path for us—if we are patient. This idea may be foreign to us because we usually operate as though we are removed from the universe. We must do, go get things and make things happen instead of allowing the process to happen. However, you are a part of a bigger picture, and with that comes trust, because no one or nothing else has power over you. It is all harmonious. There is peace when you let go and trust that the universe will unfold its path for you. We should always strive to keep our focus on what we have to do in the moment, adding something positive to the universe, and the end result will manifest itself. We tend to worry too much about the future. This worry is an indication that we do not trust that our universe will provide us for what we truly need, which is sometimes different from what we want. This wanting is attachment to the ego.

The only thing that exists is the present moment.

There is a Buddhist saying, "The secret of health for both mind and body is not to mourn for the past, worry about the future, or anticipate troubles, but to live in the present moment wisely and earnestly." One of the reasons we are distressed and not at peace is because we are not living in the present moment. We are either lamenting over the past, which creates sadness, or worrying about the future, which creates anxiety. Think about the moment that you are in at this minute. You are reading this book. The moment is (hopefully) peaceful. When is this peacefulness interrupted? Is it when you break away from the moment and start thinking about the list of things you should be doing insteadof reading? This is judging the present. Or is it when you start wondering about what needs to be done later? This is living in the future. Once you leave the moment, you are no longer feeling peaceful. When you start living in the future, you are no longer in the moment. When you are judging the moment, you are not living in the moment, because this judgment is created by past appraisals. Living in the future causes anxiety. Hurt, guilt, and resentment occur when we live in the past. Here is theirony. Both past and future do not exist. They are illusions. The only thing that truly exists is the moment that you are in right now. Yesterday only exists in our thoughts; therefore, it is not real. The future certainly does not exist. If we really think about it, how healthy is it to be preoccupied by something that does notexist-- the past and the future?

The moment is precious because that is all we really have. Ask yourself, are you frequently rushing through life, only focusing on the future? Are you judging the present moment in a critical way? Are you frequently upset about the past? It is vital to cherish every moment because there is never any certainty that there will be another. You are probably thinking: Well, what do I do if the moment is terrible? Keep in mind that it is you who are labeling it terrible. It is more appropriate to acknowledge the situation for what it is, accept it without judging, and decide what you can do right now to deal with the situation at hand. Judging your reality is only keeping you from finding peace within the moment.

One of the main reasons we are not living in the moment is because we are just thinking too much. One reason we think so much is because our mind is often times pursuing pleasure and avoiding pain in order to build a better future out of a damaged past. We think too much because we have not resolved our past and want something different for our future. It is our fear that promotes this thought process, both consciously and subconsciously. Thich Nhat Hahn reminds us: "Fear keeps us focused on the past or worried about the future. If we can acknowledge our fear, we can realize that right now we are ok. Right now, today, we are still alive, and our bodies are working marvelously. Our eyes can still see the beautiful sky."

Living in the moment is something that we need to practice with intention, and it starts by detaching from our thoughts, which takes practice. As mentioned earlier, our thoughts become addictive. You can start practicing breaking this addiction at any moment just by deciding to be in the moment. Even if you are sitting and sipping a cup of tea, do not shift to mental auto-pilot, allowing your mind to race to the past or future, but rather focus on the task at hand. Be in your body, be in the experience. If you are taking a walk, focus on what is around you, feel your body

Christina Samycia, PsyD

and feel the experience. If you notice your thoughts drifting to something other than the present, just continue refocusing your attention on it. This is called mindfulness. As you practice, it becomes easier. When a thought or negative feeling arises, this is a sign that you are not in the moment, and all you need to do is to get centered and start again. Keep in mind, we are human beings, not human doings.

The pursuit of happiness leaves us trapped in suffering.

Another paradigm shift is to focus on discovering inner peace and contentment, which will ultimately lead to joy, rather than the pursuit of happiness. Most of us are taught to pursue happiness, but this actually keeps us trapped in suffering. Happiness is a short-lived phenomenon. We can compare it to a drug because it has some similar characteristics. It allows us to escape the pain that we are feeling but, like a drug, the high wears off and we are left feeling the pain, looking for a way to avoid it. Many of us use the pursuit of happiness as a way to distract ourselves from our pain. Most of us are in pain, and no amount of money, fame, or fortune can change or mask that.

You have probably said, "I would be happy if . . . I had a better job, made more money, lost weight, etc." Now imagine obtaining that which you think would bring you happiness. Sure, you would feel happy to some degree. However, whenyou do find happiness, it cannot be sustained; like any other emotion, we can only keep it going for a short time. Another problem with the pursuit of happiness is that we tend to search for it outside ourselves. We think that someone or something, such as a pleasurable experience, an exciting activity, or a material possession will "cure" us of our unhappiness. Whenwe finally discover the object of our happiness, we find to our amazement and dismay that the pain does not necessarily go away. Furthermore, what happens if you don't get the job, you desire or find a perfect mate? You essentially give the power to an external force that may not come through for you. Your happiness is then contingent on factors that you cannot control. Seeking happiness outside ourselves gives power over us to external factors. It is difficult to find inner peace if you do not feel in control and if you are waiting for something external to make you happy. The pursuit of happiness also generally implies that it will be found in the future. This is problematic because it diminishes that happiness exists in the present. However, inner peace is something that you can experience right now, in spite of your current situation. With inner peace comes joy. Joy comes from within. It is important to pursue inner peace, which will lead you to inner joy and contentment and is something that can be achieved right now.

Reflection

We are spiritual beings having a human experience. Many things that have and are happening in your life are part of your spiritual journey. It is helpful to accept and forgive the past because these situations are part of your life journey. It is also helpful to shift from ego-based living to spiritual-based living, practice living in the moment, detaching from our thoughts, and focusing on discovering inner peace and contentment rather than the pursuit of happiness, which will ultimately lead to joy.

Part 3

Healing Your Story

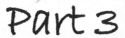

Techniques to assist in processing emotional trauma

"All know the way, but few walk it."
—Bodhidharma

Introduction to Part 3

You Have the Power to Heal Your Story and Shift Subconscious Beliefs.

Now, that you have started working on understanding your story and shifting conscious thinking, it's time for us to dig deeper and start clearing cellular memory of past trauma as well as energetically detaching from subconscious beliefs that are no longer serving you. The first section will illustrate techniques that you can do on your own. You can start by creating a self-healing practice which can include reciting affirmations, meditating, practicing self-energetic healing and so much more. These techniques can help you process emotions stored in cellular memory and shift belief systems. The second section will illustrate therapeutic techniques that you could practice with a therapist or other healing practitioner to further enhance your work such as psychotherapy, hypnotherapy, and acupuncture.

"We have learned that the key to happiness is inner peace. The greatest obstacles to inner peace are disturbed emotions such as anger, attachment, fear, and suspicion, while love and compassion and a sense of universal responsibility are the sources of peace and happiness."

—Dalai Lama

Chapter 11

Self-care Techniques

Affirmations

One of the simplest, but most effective ways to start changing your conscious and subconscious thought process is by reciting affirmations. This is a great place to start on your new self-care routine. As we have explored, you have belief systems that are stored within your conscious and subconscious mind. Therefore, the work that needs to be done is to begin reprogramming not just your conscious thinking, but more importantly, subconscious thinking. Because your subconscious mind is very susceptible to the messages it hears, if you begin saying affirmations to yourself or out loud, eventually your subconscious mind will agree with it. It might be helpful to recite affirmations everyday as a way of reprogramming your thinking.

Because self-love is so important to healing, the first affirmation that is a good place to start is "I love and accept myself." It is helpful to make a conscious effort to say this affirmation as many times as possible. It's advantageous to set aside some time in the morning and evening to practice affirmations, but they can be done at any time. Reciting affirmations may seem uncomfortable at first. When I introduce affirmation to my clients, I usually get resistance. The main response when I suggest saying "I love and accept myself," is usually "But I don't love and accept myself. How can I possibly say it?" However, it is important to start reciting affirmations even if you don't necessarily believe them. In time, your subconscious will eventually hear it enough that it will eventually agree with the statement. Remember, affirmations help reprogram the subconscious mind. Therefore, I always suggest that my clients keep saying it until they start believing it. It will work. Most of us have so many fears that impact our lives. Therefore, creating a sense of safety is also important. Another basic, yet powerful affirmation is "I am safe." Reciting this affirmation is also very helpful. Another affirmation that you can add to your daily routine is "Every day, in every way, I am getting healthier and healthier." As you continue with your affirmations, you can create your own. Keep in mind to always frame your affirmation in a positive way. Again, Louise Hay is such a great resource for other affirmations, and I would highly recommend reading her books, but the three illustrated here are a great start.

Meditation

Meditation is another very powerful tool. It is beneficial in many ways. Meditation helps us more deeply understand the different aspects of our story and detach it from it. As we have explored, we all have a script that is playing in our subconscious mind. Meditation gives us an opportunity to observe all those thoughts running in the background and to assist in detaching from them. One of the ways to achieve this is by slowing down brain processing. As mentioned earlier, our thoughts are addictive. Meditation helps in breaking this addictive pattern.

There is much research done on how meditation affects the brain in a positive way. During meditation, the frontal lobes, which are responsible for reasoning, planning, emotions and self-conscious awareness, and parietal lobes, which are responsible for processing sensory information about the surrounding world, slow down. Meditation also reduces the flow of incoming information into the thalamus, which is the gatekeeper for the senses and reduces the arousal signal of the reticular formation. When you experience a stressful situation, this triggers a reaction in the medial prefrontal cortex also referredto as the "me center." The more we meditate, the less stresswe feel because we weaken the connections of this particular neural pathway. Therefore, with meditation, we do not react as strongly to stressors as we once did. Additionally, meditation helps to strengthen our lateral prefrontal cortex also known as the "assessment center," which helps us more easily rationalize our experiences. Meditation also helps the brain switch from beta wave state, which is associated with the alert mind state ofthe prefrontal cortex, to alpha and theta states, which induces a feeling of calm and peacefulness.

It is helpful to mediate at least once or twice a day a day. Start out with 5 minutes and work your way up to 20 minutes. Find a quiet place to do your meditation practice. Get into a comfortable position. Sit with your eyes closed and make sure to keep your back straight. Start by taking in a long, slow, deep breath through your nose and then exhale out your mouth. Focus on your breathing. If a thought come into your mind, just acknowledge it and continue to focus in on your breath. You can also add a word such as peace or love or a mantra such as "I am safe," or "Breathe in and breathe out," or just focus in on your breathing as part of your meditation.

Often, when I discuss meditation with my clients, a common response is "I tried once, and I don't think I'm doing it right because I have a lot of thoughts." First, there is no wrong way to meditate because meditation is about establishing a practice. Of course, you will have thoughts while meditating. Everyone does, even experienced meditators. Meditation is not about ceasing all thoughts; it's about not attaching to them. Meditation is about practicing detaching from your thoughts. When you are focusing on your breathing and your mind wanders, just bring your attention back to your breath. It can really be that simple. Consistency is key. Even just meditating 5 minutes every day, has been shown to have positive health benefits. 5 minutes of slow deep breathing, in for 5 counts and out for 5 counts, has been shown to switch the body from a sympathetic (stressed) state to a parasympathetic (relaxed) state. Research has also shown that small segments of consistent meditation are more effective than longer periods of inconsistent meditation. You will start noticing changes once you start practicing meditation on a regular basis.

Chakra Balancing Meditation

A more advanced form of meditation is a chakra balancing meditation. There are seven chakras, or energy centers, in the body that we will focus on. Different schools of thought believe that there are more than seven. They can be described as wheels of energy located along the spine from the tip of the tailbone to the top of the head. Each chakra vibrates at a certain speed and emanates a different color. It is important that these chakras are balanced to ensure good emotional and physical health.

The first or base chakra is located at the base of the spine. It vibrates slowly, emanates a red color, and controls the consciousness of survival and the feeling of being grounded and safe. During your meditation, you can focus your attention to the base of your spine with the intention of balancing it. You can picture the color red and use the affirmation of "I am safe." The second or sacral charka is located between the base of the spine and the navel. The vibration is higher and faster than the first and the color is orange. Each chakra vibrates faster than the one before it. This chakra allows us to experience joy and physical pleasure and is responsible for our creativity. After you have aligned your first charka, in your mind's eye, focus on the second chakra with the intention of balancing it. You can picture the color orange and use the affirmation of "I am calm." The third or solar plexus chakra is located in the solar plexus, right above the navel and is the color yellow. This chakra is responsible for our personal power and sense of self. After you have aligned your first and second charka, in your mind's eye, focus on the third chakra with the intention of balancing it. You can picture the color yellow and use the affirmation of "I am powerful." Moving onto the fourth or heart chakra, this chakra is the color green and is responsible for love. The heart chakra connects the physical aspect of us with the spiritual world. In your mind's eye, imagine aligning the heart chakra with the color green and using the affirmation of "I am able to give and receive love." The fifth or throat chakra is the color blue and is responsible for expressing our personal truth. You can picture the color blue in this area and use the affirmation of "I am able to speak my truth." The sixth chakra or third eye is your intuition and the color indigo, bluish purple. As you visualize on aligning this chakra with the color indigo in mind, meditate on the affirmation "I am enhancing my intuition. The seventh or crown chakra is located on the top of the head. It is the color purple, and it connects us to the spiritual world. Instead of aligning it, focus on just opening it up and meditate on the affirmation "I am connecting to my feelings of spirituality."

Meditation with self-energy healing

Here is another exercise to clear a subconscious emotion or belief system by incorporating some energy work. First begin with an intention to heal a specific subconscious emotion or belief system such as feelings of sadness or not feeling good enough. Sit or lie in a comfortable position and enter into a deeply relaxed state. Take three deep breathes. Next, get in touch and feel the emotion in your body. You may experience sadness as a heaviness in your heart or the belief of not feeling good enough

Christina Samycia, PsyD

in your stomach, for example. Now, just pay attention to the feeling in the body. Then, imagine healing energy coming from the universe and shining a warm healing light. You can imagine white or yellow light or any other color that appears. Imagine that healing light energy absorbing the emotion or belief system.Feel the emotion or belief system start to dissolve or let go. It may create interesting sensations in your body such as tingling, warmth, or deep peace. Whatever happens, keep your focus on what is taking place. Now imagine this healing light energy taking this emotion or belief with it out into the universe far away from you and transmuting it into peace and love. Then imagine the universe infusing you with feelings of love, peace, and safety. You can also ask the universe to infuse you with whatever you wish to replace such as joy instead of sadness or feeling good enough instead of not feeling good enough. You may need to do this meditation a few times to fully let go of an emotional charge.

Emotional Freedom Technique (EFT)

Here is another powerful technique that you can try that also incorporates energy points. The premise of EFT is that the cause of all negative emotions is a disruption in the body's energy system. EFT helps clear negative emotions by tapping on energy points. It works by focusing on the specific issue you wish to change while tapping on a sequence of energy points. The first thing you are going to do is identify what you would like to clear. Then rate the distress by assigning a number to it on a 0-10 scale where 10 is the worst the issue has ever been and 0 is no problem whatsoever. Then you tap continuously on the KC (karate chop) point with your fingertips, while saying. "Even though I have this_____(feeling of sadness or belief that I'm not good enough), I deeply and completely accept myself". Say this three times while tapping continuously on the KC point.

KC: The Karate Chop point is located at the center of the fleshy part of the outside of your hand between the top of the wrist and the base of the baby finger.

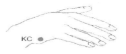

Then tap with your fingertips on the points indicated. You will tap approximately 5 times on each point. The only exception is in the beginning where the KC point is tapped continuously while you repeat the phrase you chose. The tapping is done with two or more fingertips. While you can tap with the fingertips of either hand, most people use their dominant hand. For example, right-handed people tap with the fingertips of their right hand while left-handed people tap with the fingertips of their left hand. It doesn't matter what side of the body you tap on. On the next page are the points you will tap in sequence.

Once you have completed two rounds of tapping, rate the distress again. 0-10 scale where 10 is the worst the issue has ever been and 0 is no problem whatsoever. If the distress is still there, do another round of tapping but alter the beginning phrase accordingly, such as "Even though I still feel a little sad or somewhat not good enough, I deeply and completely loveand accept myself." If it increased intensity, continue doing the tapping, altering your words, until there is relief. Continue, as necessary.

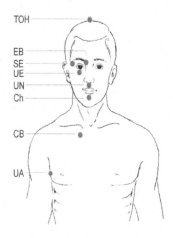

TOH: On the top of the head

EB: At the beginning of the eyebrow.

SE: On the bone bordering the outside corner of the eye.

UE: On the bone under an eye about 1 inch below your pupil.

UN: On the small area betweenthe bottom of your nose and thetop of your upper lip.

Ch: Midway between the point of your chin and the bottom of your lower lip.

CB: The junction where the sternum (breastbone), collarbone and the first rib meet. To locate it, first place your forefingeron the U-shaped notch at the top of the breastbone. From the bottom of the U, move your forefinger down 1 inch and then go to the left (or right) 1 inch.

UA: On the side of the body, at a point even with the nipple (for men) or in the middle of the bra strap (for women). It is about 4 inches below the armpit. This point is abbreviated UA for under the art.

Th: Thumb point even with the base of the nail.

IF: Index finger. Tap on the side of the finger that isclosest to the thumb, even with the base of the nail.

MF: Middle finger. Tap on the side of the finger closest to theindex finger, even with the base of the nail.

BF: Baby Finger. Tap on the side of the finger that is closest tothe ring finger, even with the base of the nail.

The Script Meditation

As mentioned previously, we all have unresolved emotions from our past and dysfunctional belief systems that are stored in our subconscious mind. Here is a "script" meditation that was edited from Feelings Buried Alive Never Die by Karol Kuhn Truman, which is another resource I highly recommend. This script meditation assists you in resolving these emotions and clearing subconscious beliefs and processing them by connecting to their origins. You can do this meditation as often as needed. Before you begin, think about a feeling or a belief system you would like to clear, such as feeling of sadness or a belief such as "I am not good enough". Then think of what you would like to feel or think instead such as "joyful" or "good enough". Get into a comfortable position. Close your eyes and take a deep breath through your nose and then exhale out your mouth. On the second and third breaths, inhale through your nose and then hold for the count of three and then exhale.

Next you will read the following script meditation: "I ask my higher self to go the beginning and locate the cause or reason for this feeling/thought of_____. (Fill in what you would like to clear, e.g., unhappiness or belief that you are not good enough) Take my subconscious self to that first situation that caused this feeling to start and analyze it perfectly. Come forward in time analyzing and resolving every similar incident built upon this first situation. Fill me with light and truth, and universal peace and love and_____. (Fill in how you would like to feel, such as happy, or think "I am good enough".) Know that every physical problem and inappropriate behavior based on the old feeling and thought quickly disappears. Take all the time you need, spirit, but quicken time and do the job now. Thank you, higher self,for coming to me and helping me attain the full measure of my creation. Thank you."

Christina Samycia, PsyD

Because you may have some self-sabotaging beliefs or blocks to changing or success, you may choose to first do the following meditation first a few times to clear them. "I ask my higher self to go the beginning and locate the cause or reason that I am programmed to fail... (and then continue the script until you get to the part where you insert how you would like to feel and then insert) I now allow myself to succeed. I give myself permission to succeed. I re-program myself to succeed. I am successful...." (and then finish the rest of the script). Because self-love and acceptance is very important, I would also suggest incorporating this statement a few times into your script meditation as well: "I ask my higher self to go the beginning and locate the cause or reason why I don't love myself... (and then continue the script until you get to the part where you insert how you would like to feel and then insert) I love myself unconditionally. I am worthy of being loved..." (and then finish the rest of the script). Add this statement, "I ask my higher self to go the beginning and locate the cause or reason why I don't accept and trust myself...(and then continue the script until you get to the part where you insert how you would like to feel and then insert) I accept myself unconditionally and trust myself implicitly. I am my own best friend..." (and then finish the rest of the script).

A good protocol would be to recite the script daily, clearing self-sabotaging blocks for a week, then recite the script daily incorporating self-love for a week, then recite the script daily incorporating accepting and trusting yourself for a week, and then finally work on any other emotions or beliefs you would like to clear such as feelings of sadness or not feeling good enough.

Healing Code Meditation

Here is another powerful meditation that was edited from The Healing Code by Alexander Loyd and Ben Johnson, another great resource. This meditation also incorporates energy points. First, get into a meditative and comfortable position. You then recite the following meditation: "I pray that all known and unknown negative images, unhealthy beliefs, destructive cellular memories, and all physical issues related to _____ (your problem or issue such as feelings of anxiety) would be found, opened, and healed by filling me with the light, life and love of the Universe. I also pray that the effectiveness of this healing be increased by 100 times or more." After you recite the meditation, you then perform three rounds of hand positions. With your fingers almost touching, you aim all five finger tips on both hands two inches away from four points for 30 seconds on each point. The points are as follows. The third eye or middle of your forehead, the Adam's apple, the bottom of the jaw and the temples. It is recommended to do this meditation 3 times a day. The meditation takes 6 minutes. It consists of four points for 30 seconds, three rounds of each. You can find more information on-line or in the book on how to perform the meditation.

Sound healing

Sound healing has been used for thousands of years. The premise of sound healing is that everything has a vibration or a sound. This sound is called resonance, the frequency in which an object naturally vibrates. Each part of our bodies has its own natural resonance. Sound therapy is based on the idea that psychological and physical ailments are a result of those natural resonances falling out of tune. There are many forms of sound therapy, such as Tibetan bowls, crystal bowls, tuning forks, gongs, chanting, binaural beats, theta healing music and so many others. The vibrations from these modalities have been shown to relax brainwave patterns, focus the mind, produce parasympathetic responses such as lower heart rate and blood pressure and decrease stress hormones. Sound healing helps facilitate shifts in our brainwaves by using entrainment. Entrainment synchronizes our fluctuating brainwaves by providing a stable frequency to which the brainwave can attune. By using rhythm and frequency, we can entrain our brainwaves to shift from normal beta waves (waking state) to alpha (relaxed state) and even reach theta wave (meditative state). Sound healing can also help in releasing energy blockages as well as emotions that are stored in the body. If you are focusing on releasing, for example, feelings of anxiety, you can use a Tibetan bowl or work with a therapist that performs sound healing.

Yoga

Most people are aware of the physical health benefits of yoga, but yoga has so many additional benefits than just increased flexibility and overall physical fitness. Yoga is effective at improving mental and emotional health. Yoga has a similar effect on the body as meditation. The practice can help you relax, while increasing your ability to focus and concentrate, which is helpful for overthinking. In yoga, when you are moving through poses, you need to focus on your pose. If your mind wanders, you will not be able to perform the pose. Yoga is a great place to start if you want to start a meditation practice. Through yoga, you learn to slow down, breathe deeply, and do one thing at a time which retrains your mind to focus on the present moment. Each movement in yoga also has a physical health benefit. Practicing a twist stimulates the digestive system. Practicing any inverted position, such as downward facing dog, stimulates the endocrine system. Yoga also has a spiritual component. Many people who practice yoga regularly feel a connection between their body, mind and spirit as well as an oneness with all. An easy way to start incorporating a simple yoga practice into your daily routine is to perform three rounds of sun salutations (see chart below), which works on all the organs of the body and is a great way to get started.

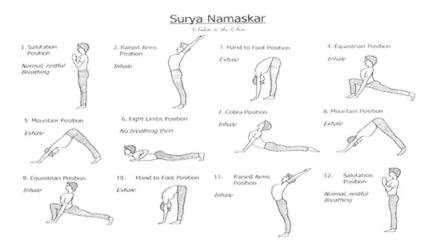

Surya Namaskar

Setting up a self-healing practice

Now that you have practiced some of the affirmations, started meditating and performed some energetic techniques such as EFT, it may be helpful to begin setting up a daily practice of healing. I will share with you my daily practice as an example. Every day, I begin my practice by taking a few cleansing breaths and then I begin to play my Tibetan bowl. You can also use a tuning fork or any sound healing instrument or music to help you get centered. I then gather up some crystals. I routinely use a large clear quartz and amethyst crystal and any other crystals that I feel may be helpful. I then begin my meditation which lasts 5-20 minutes. I either focus on slow deep breathing and/or recite a mantra. You might also want to add to your daily practice three rounds of yoga sun salutations, which can be quite helpful.

Christina Samycia, PsyD

In addition to a daily routine, I perform rituals every new and full moon as well to celebrate the change of seasons. This is a great way to spiritually connect as well as to reflect, set intentions and release things that no longer serve you. These rituals are a little more elaborate. I always start by burning sage throughout the house and then cleansing my crystals. I also play some sound healing music and light-colored candles to represent the different chakras.

The new moon represents fresh starts and beginnings. This is a good time to set intentions about what you wish to createin your life. I start by meditating. After I am centered, I usually light a white candle and then write down my intention, such asto attract anything I feel like I need in my life and sign and date it. I pick some crystals that I place on my written intention and set it aside.

The full moons are about letting go of that which no longer serves you. In addition to lighting a white candle, I also have a small bowl with water and place another empty bowl in front of me. After I am centered, I light a white candle and then write down what I wish to release from my life such as feelings of sadness or the belief that I am not good enough. I then sign and date it. I then take a deep breath and declare "I now let this go. And it is so." Then I place one corner of the piece of paper over the candle allowing the flame to light the paper. I then throw the paper into the empty bowl as it burns watching the flames consume what I am releasing and the smoke taking my intention to the Universe. I then place my hands in the bowl of water signifying cleansing of the old and opening to the new. Ithen sit in silence for a moment.

After either ritual, I always take a bath with Epsom salts and essential oils. You can choose to do the bath before the ritual. A salt bath has so many benefits. The main ingredient in Epsom salt is magnesium, which can be absorbed through the skin and is helpful in relaxing the mind and body. Additionally, salt baths are useful to help you get grounded and energetically back in balance, as well as help clear out energy. Anytime, you are doing emotional clearing, a salt bath afterwards is quite helpful. You can choose to also defuse or add to your salt bath essential oil. Frankincense is a great essential oil to use because it enhances spiritual awareness.

Chapter 12

Therapeutic Modalities

Psychotherapy

Psychotherapy is effective in helping process trauma as well as identifying and changing belief systems that are contributing to emotional distress. Because you are so close to your story, it is sometimes difficult for you to see all the subconscious belief systems you hold and to find an alternate way of perceiving reality. Here is an analogy I often use to illustrate this concept. Imagine that you are wearing a set of red-colored glasses all the time, but you are not aware that you are wearing glasses at all. Everything will be colored in red. It isn't until someone points out that you are wearing red glasses that you can actually take them off and have a different perspective. Your childhood experiences color all of your current reality, which is why it is sometimes difficult to see reality any other way. Because this can be difficult, it may be helpful to seek out assistance from a therapist. The therapist can assist you by helping you take off the red lens glasses or to help you understand how your past is coloring your present reality, so that you can see reality with clarity in a safe and non-judgmental way. Let's examine how therapy works and how this is so useful in the process of self-discovery and healing.

Therapy provides a safe place for you to explore and understand all the aspects of your story, which can be scary and overwhelming especially if you have had significant trauma in your life. The therapist can provide you with unconditional positive regard in an objective nonjudgmental fashion, which we do not usually receive from the people in our lives. The therapist can also help you identify the origins of your belief systems and perceptions that are triggering emotional pain. A therapist can help you understand how you are perceiving current reality and help you relate them to your past childhood experiences to explain why you think and feel the way you do. The therapist can also provide you with alternative ways of perceiving your past and current reality to help minimize your distress. Many therapists also are trained in techniques that help process trauma stored in cellular memory such as hypnotherapy, Neuro-emotional technique (NET), Eye Movement Desensitization and Reprogramming (EMDR), Holographic Memory resolution (HMR) and others, which will be explored in more detail later on.

In addition to exploring and understanding your story and how it impacts your present life, the therapist can also help you validate your emotions. Part of the reason why your emotions are so painful is precisely because they were not validatedduring your developmental years. When your emotions are not validated, you do not learn how to cope with them effectively, and you tend to rationalize, avoid, or suppress them. Your emotions can also be painful because you have not learned how to soothe yourself. When your feelings are not validated, it's as if they do not matter and that can make you feel as if you do not matter. If your emotions are not validated at an early age, this can create a sense of shame regarding your emotional state, and you feel misunderstood, all of which impacts your present self-esteem. You can start validating your emotions by looking at these feelings as if you were that child, looking at them in present time.

A therapist can help with that process. Sometimes it is difficult for us to validate our own feelings, which is why it is so beneficialto seek outside help. The therapist does not judge your feelings but validates them. A therapist truly listens. External validationis a very powerful tool in the healing process. This is one ofthe most powerful processes that happens in therapy and why most people feel good when they talk to a therapist. Additionally,there is a cathartic affect in just sharing the story, which is so very powerful.

Another benefit of therapy is that the therapist will encourage you to feel your feelings, which is important in processing these unprocessed emotions. When negative emotions are experienced, we tend to push them away because we are either afraid to feel them or they are too painful. When you start examining your story, it is important to really feel your emotions. You may sometimes recognize this pain, at least partially, or you may push it into your subconscious because it makes you feel uncomfortable, hurt, and vulnerable. Although we all differ in the types of experiences we encountered, we all feel the resulting emotional scars that keep resurfacing. Thatis why it is important to work through the pain. By continually working on it and through it, you can learn how to process this pain. As you work on your exercise of exploring the past, it is important that you sit with these feelings and truly feel them, andtherapy is great place to do that. When you start to feel your feelings, feel them with the understanding that soon you will let them go. They do not have to be overwhelming, because you can control the process now that you know what you are dealingwith. Feel the sadness, feel the anger, feel all the pain and, onceyou do, only then should you start to let those feelings go. Duringthis process, the therapist may start using some of the mind- body modalities that I will now illustrate to help you continue to process these emotions.

Hypnotherapy

As we have discovered, our subconscious mind is powerful. In order to facilitate real change in our behavior, it is important to make changes to the subconscious mind. Hypnotherapy is a great tool to facilitate this because it works by bypassing the conscious mind, usually through relaxation or linguistic techniques, and speaking directly to the subconscious mind. Hypnotherapy uses guided relaxation, intense concentration, and focused attention to achieve a heightened state of awareness that is sometimes called a hypnotic trance. When you are experiencing hypnosis, your attention is so focused while in this state that anything going on around you is temporarily blocked out or ignored. The hypnotic state allows you to explore painful thoughts, feelings, and memories that might have been hidden from your conscious mind, which helps to process emotions. Hypnosis is also useful in accessing and updating subconscious material, essentially reprograming the subconscious mind. Hypnosis can either be suggestive or interactive. It can also be a combination of the two. An additional benefit of hypnosis is that it is wonderful for general relaxation and helps relax the nervous system.

Neuro-Emotional Technique (NET)

"NET is a mind-body technique that uses a methodology of finding and removing neurological imbalances related to the physiology of unresolved emotional stress," www.netmindbody. com. The NET practitioner assists the client in locating unresolved emotional patterns and assists the body in processing it through either a pulse correction, which is typically used, or through a spinal correction, which is used by chiropractors. NET is based on the physiological foundations of stress-related responses. As we previously learned, the body remembers and stores traumas and compares incoming information with past experiences. According to Traditional Chinese Medicine (TCM), our bodies

Christina Samycia, PsyD

hold onto emotional responses and stores different emotions in different parts of our bodies known as meridians. For example, fear is located in the kidney meridian, anger is located in the liver meridian. If during your childhood you were exposed to a lot of yelling, this original trauma stored as fear, in the kidney meridian, and every time you are exposed to someone yelling, this triggers this fear, which stresses the kidney meridian. With a NET practitioner, you can go back to the original trauma and process the emotion so that it is no longer creating a physiological trigger by creating a pulse correction to the corresponding meridian which holds the emotion, in this case the kidney meridian. For more information regarding NET, please visit www.netmindbody.com.

Eye Movement Desensitization and Reprocessing (EMDR)

EMDR is a psychotherapy treatment that alleviates the distress associated with traumatic memories. The premise of EMDR is that the mind can heal from psychological trauma much as the body can heal from physical trauma. The brain's information processing system has a natural tendency to process trauma so that it is no longer painful, but this system can be blocked by unprocessed trauma. When the trauma is processed, natural healing occurs. The EMDR clinician uses a protocol of treatment which includes eye movements or other bilateral stimulation. The client recalls the traumatic event and uses his/her eyesto track the therapist's hand as it moves back and forth across the client's field of vision or other bilateral stimulation. The clientthen begins to process the memory and any disturbing feelings similar to what might occur during Rapid Eye Movement (REM) sleep. The client is then asked to reframe what has occurred andthe meaning of painful events is transformed. For more information, please visit www.emdr.com.

Holographic Memory Resolution (HMR)

HMR is therapeutic technique that was created by Brent Baum, an addiction counselor and clinical hypnotherapist, which is grounded in somatic and energy psychology and emphasizes the mind-body connection. The practitioner utilizes this technique to help individuals release past trauma and emotional and physical pain. Whether the trauma was a single event or repeated patterns. HMR enables individuals who have experienced trauma to access memories of these past experiences and heal from them without becoming re-traumatized or overwhelmed by painful feelings. Milton Erickson, a psychologist and hypnotherapist, suggested that emotional pain linked to past trauma could lead to a self-hypnotic state when triggered in the present. The body and mind attempt to prevent further pain by activating a state of self-hypnosis or trance states. The goal of HMR is to remove the memory storing that has taken place. By redesigning the encoding, the emotionally charged response to the memory can be altered to allow a more positive or neutral reaction.

When performing HMR, a gentle hypnotic trance is induced to allow the person's conscious mind to relax and access the subconscious. Therapists frequently use guided visualization to identify the history of the presenting issue and its emotional associations, making use of color in this process. HMR practitioners assist individuals in identifying areas of the body where difficult memories are stored and helps them release these memories through emotional reframing. Individuals are encouraged to visualize events and describe the emotions experienced through colors and symbols, reimagining painful or challenging events until they no longer have the same traumatizing effect. For more information, please visit www. healing dimensions.com.

Christina Samycia, PsyD

Energy healing

There are so many different methods of energy healing such as Acupuncture, Acupressure, Colorpuncture, bodywork such as Shiatsu and Thai massage, Breathwork and energy work such as Reiki and New Paradigm, many of which are rootedin TCM. As we have already learned, emotional and physical trauma disrupt the energetic flow in the body. According to TCM, energy or "qi" flows through the body along meridians. If this energy gets blocked, illness can occur, either physical or psychological. These energy healing methods release blocked qiand stimulate the body's natural healing response. Additionally, these techniques enhance communication between organs and cells. Acupuncture utilizes needles to facilitate this. Acupressureand bodywork techniques utilize touch. Colorpuncture utilizes colored lights instead of needles to work on acupuncture points. Breathwork, sometimes referred to as holotropic, shamanic or ecstatic breathwork, combines intense and accelerated breathing with evocative music to assist in releasing physical and emotional blocks by supercharging the body with oxygen and achieving an altered state of consciousness. Reiki andNew Paradigm are also energy healing techniques where the practitioner is able to balance the flow of energy and releases blockages through light or even no touch. All of these methods help shift energy to process stored trauma.

Reflection

There are several self-care techniques to help you change conscious and subconscious belief systems and help process trauma that is stored in cellular memory including affirmations, meditation, Chakra balancing meditations, meditation with self-energy healing, Emotional Freedom Technique, the Script Meditation, the Healing Code Meditation, sound healing and Yoga. There are other therapeutic modalities that are helpful with this process including psychotherapy, hypnotherapy, Neuro-emotional Technique, Eye Movement Desensitization and Reprogramming, Holographic Memory Resolution, and various energy healing.

Putting it All Together

You have done a lot of great work! Let's summarize what you learned. You now understand that you created inaccurate belief systems in childhood. You also now know that some of your childhood experiences created emotional trauma that is stored in your body as cellular memory, as well as other trauma from your parents, ancestors, and past lives. Hopefully, you have started writing a narrative of your story and possibly journaled your daily stressors. With this information, you have likely identified some conscious and subconscious beliefs that trigger emotional pain. Now that you have identified some stress provoking beliefs, hopefully, you have been able to update some of them to feel more empowered and less distressed. Lastly, you now have some tools to help you energetically process these stored emotions as well as detach from belief systems that are creating your suffering. You may have decided to try techniques such as EFT and the script on your own. You may have also decided to work with a therapist and try some therapeutic techniques such as NET and EMDR. I hope that you continue on your journey of self-discovery and inner peace using this book as a reference!

"Whatever you can do or dream you can, begin it. Boldness has genius, power, and magic in it."

—Goethe

Epilogue

I believe that there is a shift in consciousness occurring right now. Many of us are awakening to the state of the world we have created. It appears as though our planet is in a state of crisis. Because of this, many of us are feeling anxious, sad, angry, hopeless, and victimized. The condition of our planetcan be seen as a projection of the collective consciousness, which is illuminating the consequences of our ego-driven life. I believe that is why many of us are now exploring spirituality. Theworld appears dysfunctional as a way of illuminating our inner dysfunction. And in order to change the planet, we all need to change individually because the first step to world peace is inner peace. It is so important for each of us to truly understand that we are not victims in the world, but the creators of it. It is time for each of us to take responsibility over what we are contributing to the collective. I believe that the most important thing we can do is to evolve spiritually by working through our pain and fears, changing our dysfunctional beliefs, and becoming more mindful as to how we are living our lives. I also believe that love is the most powerful healer. By focusing on love and hope, I believe we can heal the planet. Throughout this book, I use the illustration of the drop of water falling into a pond as a metaphor of the human experience. Each of us is like a drop of water. It is a reminder that although we appear separate, we are all part of a collective.And like the drop of water that creates ripples as it flows back toits source, we have the power to affect the world around us.

"Be the change you wish to see in the world."
—Gandhi

References

Adler, A. (1927) Understanding Human Nature. New York: Greenberg.

Arntz, W., Chasse, B. and Vincente, M. (2005) What the bleep do we know!?: Discovering the endless possibilities for altering your everyday reality. Deerfield Beach, FL: Health communications.

Chopra, D. (1989) Quantum healing: Exploring the frontier of the mind/body. New York, NY: Bantam Books.

Choquette, S. (1994) The psychic pathway. New York, NY: Harmony Books.

Croke, M. (2016) Energy psychology. Using light and color. Boulder, CO: Points of Light Press.

Freud (1937) The ego and the mechanism of defense, London; Hogarth Press and Institute of Psycho-Analysis.

Hay, L. (2013) The essential Louise Hay collection. New York, NY: Hay House.

Lipton, B. (2005) The biology of belief: Unleashing the power of consciousness, matter and miracles. New York, NY: Hay House.

Peck, M. S. (1978) The road less traveled: A new psychology of love, traditional values, and spiritual growth. New York, NY: Simon and Schuster.

Peck, M. S. (1997) The road less traveled and beyond: spiritual growth in an age of anxiety. New York, NY: Touchstone.

Redfield, J. (1999) Celestine vision. New York, NY: Grand Central Publishing.

Ruiz, M. (1997) The four agreements. A practical guide to personal freedom. San Rafael, CA: Amber-Allen Publisher.

Tolle, E. (2005) A New Earth; awakening to your life's purpose. New York, NY: Dutton/Penguin Group.

Truman, K. (1991) Feelings Buried Alive Never Die. Las Vegas, NV: Olympus Distributing.

Weiss, B. (1988) Many lives, many masters. New York, NY. Simon and Schuster.

Weiss, B. (2000) Messages from the masters. Tapping into the power of love. New York, NY: Warner Books.

Yalom, I. (1980) Existential psychotherapy. New York, NY: Basic Books.

Yalom, I. (2002) The gift of therapy; an open letter to a new generation of therapists and their patients. New York, NY: Harper Collins.

Made in United States
Orlando, FL
30 August 2023

36566408R00085